DATE DUE

GAYLORD			PRINTED IN U.S.A.

The Immune System

THE HUMAN BODY
How It Works

The Immune System

Gregory J. Stewart, Ph.D.

INTRODUCTION BY

Denton A. Cooley, M.D.
President and Surgeon-in-Chief
of the Texas Heart Institute
Clinical Professor of Surgery at the
University of Texas Medical School, Houston, Texas

CHELSEA HOUSE
PUBLISHERS
An imprint of Infobase Publishing

Chelsea House
An imprint of Infobase Publishing
132 West 31st Street
New York NY 10001

Library of Congress Cataloging-in-Publication Data

Stewart, Gregory John.
  The immune system / by Gregory J. Stewart
      p. cm. — (The human body, how it works)
  Includes bibliographical references and index.
  ISBN 978-1-60413-372-1 (hardcover)
  1. Immune system—Juvenile literature. I. Title. II. Series.

  QR181.8.S743 2009
  616.07'9—dc22   2009013064

Chelsea House books are available at special discounts when purchased in bulk
quantities for businesses, associations, institutions, or sales promotions. Please call
our Special Sales Department in New York at (212) 967-8800 or (800) 322-8755.

You can find Chelsea House on the World Wide Web at
http://www.chelseahouse.com

Series design by Erika Arroyo, Erik Lindstrom
Cover design by Takeshi Takahashi

Printed in the United States of America

Bang EJB 10 9 8 7 6 5 4 3 2

This book is printed on acid-free paper.

All links and Web addresses were checked and verified to be correct at the time of
publication. Because of the dynamic nature of the Web, some addresses and links may
have changed since publication and may no longer be valid.

Contents

Introduction

THE HUMAN BODY IS AN INCREDIBLY COMPLEX AND amazing structure. At best, it is a source of strength, beauty, and wonder. We can compare the healthy body to a well-designed machine whose parts work smoothly together. We can also compare it to a symphony orchestra in which each instrument has a different part to play. When all of the musicians play together, they produce beautiful music.

From a purely physical standpoint, our bodies are made mainly of water. We are also made of many minerals, including calcium, phosphorous, potassium, sulfur, sodium, chlorine, magnesium, and iron. In order of size, the elements of the body are organized into cells, tissues, and organs. Related organs are combined into systems, including the musculoskeletal, cardiovascular, nervous, respiratory, gastrointestinal, endocrine, and reproductive systems.

Our cells and tissues are constantly wearing out and being replaced without our even knowing it. In fact, much of the time, we take the body for granted. When it is working properly, we tend to ignore it. Although the heart beats about 100,000 times per day and we breathe more than 10 million times per year, we do not normally think about these things. When something goes wrong, however, our bodies tell us through pain and other symptoms. In fact, pain is a very effective alarm system that lets us know the body needs attention. If the pain does not go away, we may need to see a doctor. Even without medical help, the body has an amazing ability to heal itself. If we cut ourselves, the blood-clotting system works to seal the cut right away, and the immune defense system sends out special blood cells that are pro-grammed to heal the area.

During the past 50 years, doctors have gained the ability to repair or replace almost every part of the body. In my own field of cardiovascular surgery, we are able to open the heart and repair its valves, arteries, chambers, and connections. In many cases, these repairs can be done through a tiny "keyhole" incision that speeds up patient recovery and leaves hardly any scar. If the entire heart is diseased, we can replace it altogether, either with a donor heart or with a mechanical device. In the future, the use of mechanical hearts will probably be common in patients who would otherwise die of heart disease.

Until the mid-twentieth century, infections and contagious diseases related to viruses and bacteria were the most common causes of death. Even a simple scratch could become infected and lead to death from "blood poisoning." After penicillin and other antibiotics became available in the 1930s and 1940s, doctors were able to treat blood poisoning, tuberculosis, pneumonia, and many other bacterial diseases. Also, the introduction of modern vaccines allowed us to prevent childhood illnesses, smallpox, polio, flu, and other contagions that used to kill or cripple thousands.

Today, plagues such as the "Spanish flu" epidemic of 1918–19, which killed 20 to 40 million people worldwide, are unknown except in history books. Now that these diseases can be avoided, people are living long enough to have long-term (chronic) conditions such as cancer, heart failure, diabetes, and arthritis. Because chronic diseases tend to involve many organ systems or even the whole body, they cannot always be cured with surgery. These days, researchers are doing a lot of work at the cellular level, trying to find the underlying causes of chronic illnesses. Scientists recently finished mapping the human genome, which is a set of coded "instructions" programmed into our cells. Each cell contains 3 billion "letters" of this code. By showing how the body is made, the human genome will help researchers prevent and treat disease at its source, within the cells themselves.

The body's long-term health depends on many factors, called risk factors. Some risk factors, including our age, sex, and family history of certain diseases, are beyond our control. Other important risk factors include our lifestyle, behavior, and environment. Our modern lifestyle offers many advantages but is not always good for our bodies. In western Europe and the United States, we tend to be stressed, overweight, and out of shape. Many of us have unhealthy habits such as smoking cigarettes, abusing alcohol, or using drugs. Our air, water, and food often contain hazardous chemicals and industrial waste products. Fortunately, we can do something about most of these risk factors. At any age, the most important things we can do for our bodies are to eat right, exercise regularly, get enough sleep, and refuse to smoke, overuse alcohol, or use addictive drugs. We can also help clean up our environment. These simple steps will lower our chances of getting cancer, heart disease, or other serious disorders.

These days, thanks to the Internet and other forms of media coverage, people are more aware of health-related matters. The average person knows more about the human body than ever before. Patients want to understand their medical conditions and treatment options. They want to play a more active role, along with their doctors, in making medical decisions and in taking care of their own health.

I encourage you to learn as much as you can about your body and to treat your body well. These things may not seem too important to you now, while you are young, but the habits and behaviors that you practice today will affect your physical well-being for the rest of your life. The present book series, THE HUMAN BODY: HOW IT WORKS, is an excellent introduction to human biology and anatomy. I hope that it will awaken within you a lifelong interest in these subjects.

Denton A. Cooley, M.D.
President and Surgeon-in-Chief
of the Texas Heart Institute
Clinical Professor of Surgery at the
University of Texas Medical School, Houston, Texas

1

How Important Is the Immune System?

INTRODUCTION

YOU ARE PROBABLY FAMILIAR WITH MANY SYSTEMS OF THE HUMAN body. The skeletal system includes the bones of the body, which serve to support and protect the rest of the body. The muscular system allows the body to move, and the digestive system allows us to take in food and convert it to forms needed to build and maintain the body. It is relatively easy to understand the functions and the importance of these systems, but what about the immune system? The immune system is extremely important to us. It is the most important system in the body for avoiding and fighting infections. It also prevents the development of certain types of cancer. To help you understand the importance of this system, we will consider two examples of conditions where the immune system does not function properly. When we understand how problems with the immune system result in these conditions, we will have a better appreciation of why an effective immune system is so important to our health and well-being.

PLAGUES AND HISTORY

Every historical age of human history seems to be defined by one or more catastrophic diseases. In medieval Europe, "the black plague," or bubonic plague, was a recurring disease. Outbreaks occurred in villages and cities throughout Europe and, in many cases, were responsible for the death of up to 25% of the total population. The history of sub-Saharan Africa is marked with cycles of malaria, a disease transmitted by mosquitoes. During periods of exploration and colonization, Europeans traveling to faraway places brought home with them exotic products, such as new fruits, silks, and spices, but they also returned with previously unknown diseases, including syphilis.

Tuberculosis was the principal plague of the Romantic and Victorian periods in England's history. This wasting disease was so prevalent that it became a central and recurring theme in much of the literature of the time. When you hear of a character suffering from or dying of "consumption," the author is referring to tuberculosis. Not surprisingly, human history before the modern age is punctuated with references to these and other devastating human diseases.

We are able to find examples of diseases that altered events in the history of the Western Hemisphere. Native American populations were free of many of the traditional European diseases, and, as a result, these populations were extremely sensitive to exposure to those diseases. Franco Pizzaro and the conquistadors, who conquered and colonized much of Central and South America, were known to give "gifts" to the native populations. In many cases these gifts were laden with the virus that causes smallpox, and many historians attribute the fall of the Incan empire, one of the most advanced and sophisticated societies of human history, to the devastating effects of this early form of biological warfare. Similar strategies were used to weaken the Native American populations of North America, allowing the settlers from Europe to easily capture the lands of the Native American tribes. At the turn of the twentieth century, it was common for parents to have large families of six or more children largely due to the fact that at least one in four of those children would die from diseases such as influenza, measles, and scarlet fever. During the 1920s and through the 1940s, the United States was devastated by polio, a disease that killed many and left many of its other victims partially paralyzed.

THE PLAGUE OF THE MODERN AGE: AIDS

If there is a plague of our modern age, it is probably **acquired immune deficiency syndrome**, or **AIDS**. Although this condition will be discussed in detail in later chapters, we will discuss the disease in brief terms here, focusing on its history and its interaction with the immune system.

AIDS is a global epidemic (Figure 1.1). We are aware of its significance within the United States, but there are areas of the world where AIDS is a much more serious epidemic. In certain villages in southern Africa, as much as 95% of the adult population is HIV-positive (HIV+). **HIV**, or the **human immunodeficiency virus**, is the causative agent for AIDS. Globally, millions of people are victims of this disease. It is a slow, progressive disease that is first indicated by rather mild symptoms that are easily confused with a cold or the flu. As the disease progresses, the symptoms become much worse; the patient will be chronically ill and will begin to lose weight. In Africa, where HIV is thought to have originated, the general deterioration of health, coupled with the rapid loss of weight, has given rise to the nickname "the wasting disease," for the progressive deterioration of health associated with cases of AIDS.

Contrary to what some people believe, AIDS is a disease that should concern us all. It is not a "gay" disease or a "drug user" disease, although the disease in the United States first appeared in these populations. HIV does not discriminate. It is a disease of men and women, gay persons and heterosexuals, athletes and addicts. The history of AIDS in the United States is an interesting one. The highlights of this history follow.

The History of AIDS in the United States

To fully appreciate why and how the United States reacted to the first cases of AIDS, it is important to consider the success

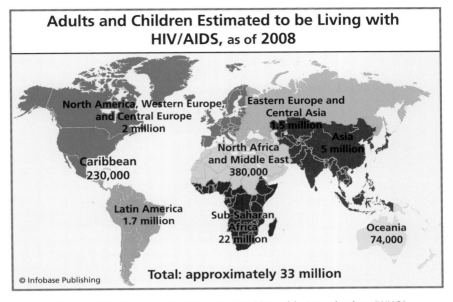

Figure 1.1 Data provided by the World Health Organization (WHO) on the global distribution of HIV/AIDS (shown here) indicates that the disease has now spread around the world. The disease can be passed through sexual intercourse (both heterosexual and homosexual) and through the transfer of blood and other bodily fluids.

made in the battle against infectious diseases in the two to three decades that preceded the AIDS epidemic. During the 1960s and 1970s, great advances were made in the area of infectious disease. Smallpox, once one of the most feared diseases in the world, had been completely eliminated. The United States was well on its way to eradicating another devastating disease, tuberculosis. We were successfully managing so many diseases with **vaccines** and antibiotics that some of the leading scientists of the time were suggesting that medical microbiology would soon become an extinct area of study. Colleges and universities that trained microbiologists began to reduce the emphasis on disease and increase the emphasis on biochemistry, molecular genetics, and environmental microbiology. As had happened so often in human history, we became overconfident in our success. Not surprisingly, when new cases of unexplained infections began to occur in 1981, we were unprepared to deal with this new crisis.

The history of AIDS in the United States built slowly. In June of 1981, a report appeared in a weekly paper published by the Centers for Disease Control and Prevention (CDC). This weekly report, known as *Morbidity and Mortality Weekly Report* (MMWR), is the most important tool for communicating information about diseases, illnesses, and accidents that affect human health. This particular issue reported that five young men from Los Angeles were treated at three different hospitals in the Los Angeles area for a type of pneumonia called *Pneumocystis carinii* pneumonia (PCP). These men appeared to be in good health, which was unexpected because this form of pneumonia is usually seen only in people who are so ill that their immune systems are not functioning properly. The men did not know each other, and their only common characteristic was that they were gay. Laboratory blood work indicated that all five men had an unusually low level of a kind of white blood cell called the **T-helper cell**, or T_H cell. As you will learn in later chapters, T-helper cells, a type of lymphocyte, are essential for activating the immune response. With such low levels of T-helper cells in the blood, the bodies of these five men could not fight the *Pneumocystis carinii* microbes in their lungs, thus causing fluid to accumulate in the lung tissue (i.e., pneumonia).

One month later, in July of 1981, the MMWR reported 26 cases of Kaposi's sarcoma (Figure 1.2), which is a cancer of the lining of the blood vessels. As the tumors grow, the walls of the blood vessels weaken and blood leaks into the surrounding tissues, causing reddish-purple patches that are visible under the skin. All 26 cases were young men: 20 men lived in New York and 6 lived in California. Again, all of these men were gay and until recently had been in good health. Before this outbreak, Kaposi's sarcoma was known to occur

Figure 1.2   Kaposi's sarcoma, a form of cancer of the lining of the blood vessels, is associated with HIV/AIDS. As tumors develop in the lining of the blood vessels, the vessels leak blood into the tissues, resulting in a dark patch like the one seen here.

only in older men of Mediterranean descent. Ten of these 26 patients also had PCP, and several others had diseases usually seen only in persons who are severely immunocompromised (having immune systems that do not function properly). A number of explanations were given for these unusual cases in young gay men; however, some believe that the government was slow to respond to these diseases because all the patients diagnosed with these cases were gay. Later in 1981, the CDC reported cases of PCP in heroin addicts and other intravenous (IV) drug users. By early the next year, the first case of transmission between heterosexuals was reported. When immune deficiency began to appear in hemophiliacs and other persons who received blood transfusions in late 1982, the public health community became concerned. This was no longer a "gay" disease. It was appearing in the broader population, and it appeared that even the United States blood supply might be contaminated with the unknown agent that was destroying the immune system of more and more Americans.

Cases of the disease, now known as AIDS, began to increase very rapidly in the United States. Shortly thereafter, cases began to appear in other countries as well. A test had been developed to detect the virus that caused the disease, but there was still no cure. Some of the patients first diagnosed began to get progressively sicker and died after months of suffering. The World Health Organization (WHO), a branch of the United Nations, was charted to address global health issues. It began to hold annual meetings to monitor and report on the disease. At the Tenth International Conference on AIDS, held in 1994, some staggering statistics were revealed. It was estimated that worldwide there might be as many as 14 million persons infected with HIV. In some villages in Africa, nearly 95% of the adult population, both men and women, were suspected of being HIV-positive. Infected women were transmitting the virus to their unborn children at alarming rates. When the infected children were born, they were weak and sick. Most died by age two. We now believe that as many as 40 million people have the disease and that it will continue to be a major health problem for at least the next 100 years.

There are still many unanswered questions about the disease. We do not know how the virus found its way into the human population, nor do we know its original host. We know, however, that the disease was probably in the United States before 1981. Tissue samples that had been frozen from autopsies of persons who died of unusual pneumonias were thawed and tested with the diagnostic kit for HIV. These tests were positive. The susceptible populations have also changed. In the early 1980s, the majority of cases were in men, particularly gay men, in IV drug users, and in both male and female prostitutes. Now researchers find the rates of new cases growing most rapidly in the heterosexual female population. The disease is known to be transmitted by sexual activity and by the transfer of blood and other bodily fluids. It is not transmitted by breathing or casual contact. HIV attacks the T-helper cells that are essential to the body's ability to raise an immune response. Without these cells, we cannot fight infection or control certain rare forms of cancer.

AIDS demonstrates the importance of our immune system. Without it, we are easy prey to disease-causing **microorganisms** and our own body's cells that mutate and become cancerous. We are making progress in the fight against AIDS. New drug therapies and other medical treatments allow AIDS patients to live longer lives of quality and dignity. Each year, the treatments improve so that AIDS patients can live longer, more productive lives. Unfortunately, these treatments only slow the progress of AIDS. Eventually the HIV virus will win and AIDS patients will die, often in the prime of their lives.

We have learned an important lesson about our bodies from those who have suffered with this disease. The immune system is essential for our survival. It protects us from infection and it controls certain types of cancer. As a result, we live longer, healthier, happier lives.

ALLERGIC REACTIONS AND AUTOIMMUNE DISEASES

Clearly, we need our immune system. Without it, we could not survive for long. AIDS shows what can happen when the immune system is underactive, but there are times when the immune system is overactive—when it harms us rather than helps us. If you suffer from watery eyes, sneezing, and a stuffy nose every spring or fall, your doctor may have told you that you have hay fever. This is an allergic reaction to pollen, dust, or spores that are present in the air. An allergic reaction is one in which your immune system reacts to foreign materials that you encounter in your everyday life—materials that do not cause problems for most people. Your immune system attacks these foreign materials, and the result is swollen and itchy tissue in your nose and eyes. Another example of the immune system working against you is a reaction to poison ivy (Figure 1.3). This plant secretes an oil that is very reactive to your immune system. When the oil gets on your skin, you get a localized reaction caused by your immune system that results in a red rash and itching.

Allergic reactions are often bothersome but only occasionally life-threatening. There are other conditions in which the immune system causes problems that are much more serious. One of the wonderful and amazing things about the immune system is that it can differentiate between our own cells and tissues and those that are "foreign." The body's ability to attack foreign materials but not its own is due to a function known as *suppression*. The body suppresses immune reactions against its own cells but attacks other things, such as bacteria, viruses, and even cancer cells. Sometimes, however, our immune system does not recognize our own tissues and begins attacking those tissues. Children with juvenile diabetes have a genetic defect that allows the immune system to attack the cells in the pancreas that produce insulin. Insulin is a hormone that is essential for maintaining the proper level of sugar in the blood. Without insulin, diabetics cannot use sugar properly, and they can therefore become very ill or even die when the sugar levels are too high.

Once the insulin-producing cells of the pancreas are destroyed by the immune system, usually around age five or six, the diabetic person must take regular injections of insulin to maintain normal blood sugar levels. A diabetic patient

Figure 1.3 Plants such as poison ivy, poison oak, and poison sumac contain a large molecule called urushiol, which is secreted from the plant as an oil. Urushiol contains many different antigenic sites. As a result, almost everyone is allergic to these plants. Poison ivy cannot be transferred from person to person, but it can be picked up from clothing that is contaminated with the oil.

may have to take several insulin injections a day. The amount of insulin taken is critical because too much insulin, like too little insulin, can lead to death. Juvenile diabetes, also called Type I or insulin-dependent diabetes, is an autoimmune disease because the immune system attacks the cells of its own body. Other examples of autoimmune diseases are rheumatoid arthritis, where the immune system attacks the soft tissues that line and cushion the joints, and lupus, where the immune system attacks the connective tissue of the skin. Later in this book, we will explore autoimmune diseases and other health problems caused by the immune system in more detail.

CONNECTIONS

What can we learn from these two very different problems—underactive and overactive immune systems? On the one hand, the immune system can become underactive when a virus damages critical cells. On the other hand, certain conditions can cause the immune system to become overactive and to attack the body, thus causing sickness and, potentially, death. The fact that the immune system functions normally for the vast majority of people indicates that it has evolved to be very finely tuned and to function optimally. The remaining chapters in this book will help you to understand how the immune system works. It is an intricate and elegant system that is essential for our survival. As we explore the immune system in greater detail you will see why many scientists consider it to be the most complex and surprising system in the human body.

2

Innate Immunity and Defenses

GENERAL TYPES OF INNATE IMMUNITY

IN SUBSEQUENT CHAPTERS OF THIS BOOK WE WILL LEARN ABOUT the amazingly complex nature of the human immune system. Some of the immune responses are so specific that they can easily distinguish one type of bacterium from another or one cell type from another. This specific form of immunity is often referred to as **acquired immunity** because it is activated only by the first exposure to a foreign microorganism or to a vaccine. This ability to mount an attack against a specific foreign invader is one of the most fascinating and complex processes of our bodies. As important as these acquired reactions are, there is another aspect of our defense that is just as important. This collection of protective defenses is referred to as the innate, or inborn, defense mechanisms. The **innate immune system** is always turned on and defends us against harmful things our bodies have never seen before. These innate defenses are so important we could not live without them.

We will discuss these innate defense mechanisms in two categories. The first, the **passive barrier defenses**, protect us by blocking the entry of harmful things, such as bacteria, fungi, viruses, and toxins, into the deeper tissues of our bodies where they could do a great deal of damage. Barrier defenses perform the same function as a moat and the reinforced walls that surround a castle. Their purpose is to keep the enemy out. The second category of innate mechanisms is the **nonspecific reactive responses**. These defenses aggressively attack foreign material that invades the body. Using our castle analogy, these defenses would be equivalent to the soldiers who fight back the invaders that manage to get past the barrier defenses. As you will see, these fighting soldiers have an extensive arsenal of weapons they can use to keep the invaders out.

Barrier Defenses

The barrier defenses are those layers on the outer surface of the body that protect the deeper tissues. The skin is one of the most important barrier defenses, and the largest organ of the body. It is made up of cells called **epithelial cells** (Figure 2.1). The design of the skin is critical to its role as a barrier. First of all, the epithelial cells are very geometric in shape. They fit together with virtually no spaces between the cells, making the layers of the skin very impermeable and hard to penetrate. Because the gaps between the cells are so small, even microorganisms cannot pass between skin cells. A second important aspect of skin structure is that it is multilayered. The layers cover each other, with the newest cell furthest from the outside of the body. As a skin layer moves toward the outside, it ages and eventually the cells in that layer die. In fact, the outermost layer of the skin is covered with dried, dead cells that are continuously shed. If a microorganism found a way to attach itself to the outer surface of the skin, it would attach to dead skin cells that would fall away; consequently, the microorganism would probably be shed before it could enter the body.

The second important barrier defense is the **mucous membranes**. These membranes are found lining the tracts of the body (the respiratory tract, the digestive tract, etc.). Mucous membranes are also made of epithelial cells, but of a different sort than skin. Skin is designed to be impermeable—that is,

Figure 2.1 Cuboidal epithelial cells of the skin are packed tightly together, keeping moisture in the body and preventing microorganisms from entering into deeper tissues. An intact skin layer is the first—and one of the best—defenses against infection.

so nothing can get through it. However, In order for the body to get nutrients, fluids, and oxygen, and to dispose of urine and fecal material, membranes must be selectively permeable. Consequently, the membranes are made of epithelial cells that are more loosely packed than are skin epithelial cells. By design it would be much easier for foreign objects to cross the membranes, especially small objects like microorganisms, but the membranes have another feature that acts as a barrier. Throughout the mucous membranes are specialized cells called goblet cells. These cells produce and secrete a sticky, thick liquid, **mucus**, onto the surface of the membranes. The mucus keeps the membranes moist and also traps foreign matter (dust, soot, and microorganisms.) The mucus acts rather like fly paper. Foreign matter becomes trapped in the gooey, sticky mucus and cannot get down to the surface of the membrane itself. Other cells that line the mucous membranes have cilia, small hairlike extensions that sweep the mucus and its trapped material toward the exits of the body. Thus, the mucous membranes also serve as a strong barrier to keep foreign matter out of the deeper tissues.

Because of the continuous barrier created by the skin and mucous membranes, most harmful microorganisms (bacteria, fungi, protozoa, and viruses) are kept on the surface of the body or lining of the cavities of the body within the mucous membranes. These areas are often teeming with microorganisms, while the tissue below these barriers (the internal organs, muscles, blood, etc.) are generally sterile (free of microorganisms) in healthy individuals.

There are areas of the body that are not protected by the skin or mucous membrane barrier. The eyes are soft tissues of the body that are exposed to the outside without protection from skin or mucous membranes. The eyes cannot be covered by these layers because if they were, you would not be able to see. Instead, the eyes have their own unique forms of defense. In the inside corners of your eyes, near the nose, there are small openings called **tear ducts**. The tear ducts continually secrete tears that wash the eyes, removing microorganisms before they can penetrate into the soft tissue of the eyeball. A second important defense for the eyes is **lysozyme**, an enzyme secreted with tears. Lysozyme attacks bacterial cell walls, weakening them so that the bacterial cells lyse, or rupture. Between the flushing action of tears and the high concentrations of lysozyme, the eyes are well protected and seldom become infected unless a large load of foreign material is introduced into them at one time.

Nonspecific Reactive Responses

Although the barrier defenses are very effective, sometimes foreign materials do manage to get around these protective barriers and enter the deeper tissues of the body. These tissues are usually warm, nutrient-rich environments that allow microorganisms to multiply rapidly. Our bodies have developed additional general defense mechanisms to deal with microbes that manage to make it to the deeper tissues. Generally, these defenses are active, aggressive ones. They seek out the invading foreigner and eliminate it. In the remainder of this chapter we will explore several of these defenses. We refer to them as nonspecific reactive responses. They are "nonspecific" because they typically attack anything that is recognized as foreign. They are "reactive" because they actively attempt to remove foreign material.

Inflammatory Response

The **inflammatory response** is a complex series of reactions that almost always occur when foreign material enters the deeper tissues of the body. We can illustrate the important parts of the inflammatory response through a specific example that you have probably experienced. Imagine you are on a farm and you decide to climb from the first floor of the barn into the hayloft. You reach for the wooden ladder that is made of unfinished wood, and as your hand slides along the rung, you feel a sharp stick. When you look at your palm, you see that a small splinter of wood has come off the rung of the ladder and is now below the surface of your skin. You cannot get the splinter out, but because it does not hurt too much, you decide to continue to explore the barn. Soon you forget that the splinter is in your palm.

The next morning you get out of bed and head downstairs, but as you grasp the handrail of the stairs, you feel a throbbing pain in your hand. When you look at your palm you see that the area around the splinter is swollen and red. As you touch it gently with your finger, you find that it is warmer than the rest of your hand and that it is sore. Your palm is displaying the classic symptoms of an inflammatory response (Figure 2.2).

Inflammation results in swelling, redness, heat, and soreness at the injured site. All of these symptoms are the result of increased blood flow to the wounded area and to

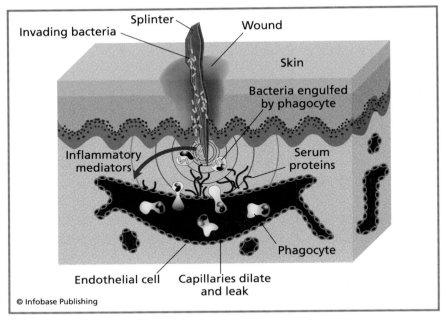

Figure 2.2   When the skin is penetrated, the damaged skin cells release inflammatory mediators that begin the acute inflammatory response. The dilation of blood vessels increases in the area, causing fluids and cells from the circulatory system to infuse the tissues around the wound. The injured site becomes warm, red, swollen, and painful. The inflammatory mediators attract immune-active cells to the site to fight infection.

the leakage of fluid from the blood vessels into the tissues around the wound. What causes these symptoms to occur? When cells are damaged, as are the cells that were penetrated by the splinter, they release chemicals known as **inflammatory mediators**. The outer surfaces of many bacteria also contain chemicals that serve as inflammatory mediators, and the splinter that penetrated through the protective barrier of your skin probably contained millions of bacteria. These inflammatory mediators have two important functions. First, they cause the capillaries in the area of the wound to dilate or become leaky. Fluid seeps from the circulatory system into the tissues around the wounded site. This results in the swelling that occurs. Because the fluid is mostly water and water holds heat well, the increase in fluid also accounts for the heat you feel at the site. The redness is caused by movement of blood cells into the affected area. The pain is the result of the extra fluid's increasing pressure at the site, which stimulates pressure-sensitive nerves. The second function of inflammatory mediators is to recruit other cells that are important in the immune response.

Inflammation has several benefits. First, the buildup of fluid may actually push the splinter out of the wound. This eliminates many of the bacteria and reduces the chance for infection. Second, as the fluid leaks into the site, it brings with it proteins called **antibodies**. These antibodies attach to molecules on the foreign materials called antigens; the bound antibodies act as tags for both white blood cells and a class of proteins called **complement proteins**. Both will ultimately eliminate bacteria from the site. Third, as the capillaries become leaky, phagocytic white blood cells leave the circulatory system and enter the tissues. These cells then engulf foreign materials and chemically destroy them.

Inflammation almost always occurs when there is injury or infection to the human body. For example, when you get a sore throat, it becomes hot and red because the tissues become inflamed. As the tissues swell, the opening of the throat gets smaller. This is why it is often hard to swallow when you have a sore throat. In almost all cases when you are sick or injured and when the area that is affected becomes sore, it is the result of inflammation.

PHAGOCYTIC CELLS

Phagocytic cells, or **phagocytes**, are a subgroup of the white blood cells. ("Phagocytosis" means "cell eating.") These cells travel through the tissues of the body and search for foreign materials, including microorganisms. When they find something that should not be there, they attach to the foreign material and engulf it by surrounding it and enclosing it within the cell membrane of the phagocyte. This process is called **phagocytosis** (Figure 2.3). The membrane of the phagocytic cell then fuses to trap the foreign material inside a sphere of membrane called a *phagosome*, which is like a bubble inside the cell. There are other membrane-enclosed structures inside the phagocytic cell that contain very powerful enzymes and chemicals. The chemical- or enzyme-containing structures fuse with the phagosome so that the contents of the two mix. The result is that the enzymes and chemicals destroy the foreign material. If that foreign material is a microorganism, the chemical or enzyme treatment kills it and makes it fall apart. This prevents it from reproducing in the body and therefore helps avoid infection.

You have phagocytic white blood cells in virtually all tissues of your body, but some tissues have more than others. For instance, your lungs are a site where the mucous membranes have to be relatively thin and free of mucus. This is essential because the tiny sacs in the lungs, the alveoli, are the sites where oxygen and carbon dioxide are exchanged with the blood. If the membranes were too thick or the layer of mucus too heavy, the exchange of respiratory gases could not occur efficiently. The alveoli have large numbers of specialized phagocytes called alveolar **macrophages** ("macrophage" means a "big, eating cell.") The alveolar macrophages move throughout the alveoli engulfing and destroying any foreign material, including microorganisms, that may make it into the deepest parts of the lungs. There are also large numbers of phagocytic cells in **lymphatic tissues**, including the tonsils and the lymph nodes. Lymphatic tissues and organs are discussed in the next chapter.

In addition to phagocytic cells, the body contains other immune-active cells that are attracted to infected tissues, but we will discuss these in more detail later.

COMPLEMENT PROTEINS

One of the most interesting and complicated of the nonspecific, reactive defenses is the **complement system**. Complement

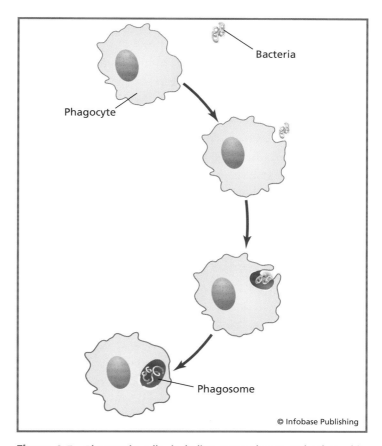

Figure 2.3 Phagocytic cells, including macrophages and other white blood cells, recognize antibodies or binding sites on the surface of foreign materials and bind to them. The phagocytic cell then extends its cell membrane around both sides of the foreign material until the two "arms" of the cell meet. These arms fuse together, trapping the foreign material in a special vesicle called a phagosome. The phagosome then fuses with other vesicles in the phagocytic cell, and powerful enzymes and other chemicals break down the foreign materials into small pieces.

proteins are found in the blood. Although we do not know the exact number, there may be as many as 60 different proteins that make up the complement system. These proteins work through a sequence, or cascade, of reactions. One or a few of the complement proteins act first; then another group is activated, then another, and another, until finally the foreign material is destroyed. Complement proteins seem to be most important in fighting bacterial infections, but unlike antibodies, which are also proteins found in the blood, complement proteins attack any kind of bacteria, whereas each type of antibody generally attack only a single bacterial species. There are several different complement pathways. The two we will mention here are the classical complement pathway and the alternate complement pathway.

The **classical complement pathway** (Figure 2.4) requires the involvement of antibodies. When antibodies bind to a microorganism, such as a bacterium, sections of the antibody protein extend out from the bacterial cell. One of the complement proteins binds to the free ends of the antibody molecule. The complement protein then changes shape and becomes the binding site for other complement proteins. These new complement proteins bind to the first protein, and the new proteins split. One piece remains attached to the bacterial cell while the other floats away and becomes both an inflammatory mediator and an attracting agent for immune system cells. The fragments of the second round of complement proteins bind and alter other complement proteins. These proteins embed in the wall of the bacterial cell and eventually form a hole in the cell. The hole is completely surrounded by a ring of complement proteins. Once this hole is formed, fluids rush into the bacterial cell, causing it to explode.

The **alternate complement pathway** results in the same fate for the bacterium: A ring of complement proteins creates a hole in the bacterial cell. The hole results in lysis (bursting) and killing of the cell, but the alternate pathway does not require antibody molecules. The surfaces of certain bacterial cells have specific molecules that bind complement proteins on their own. Once these proteins bind, they start the complement cascade of binding and splitting complement proteins until the complement ring punches a hole in the bacterial cell, leading to its death.

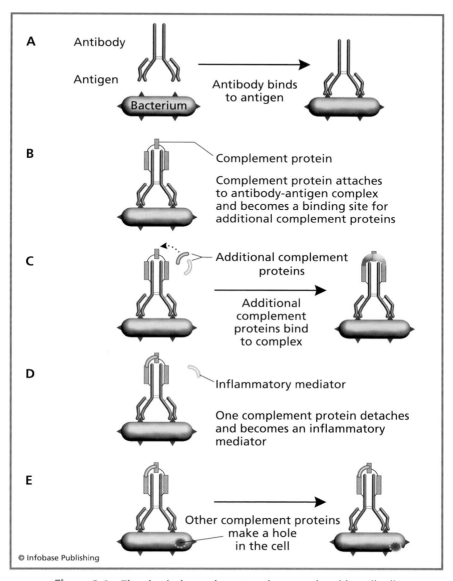

A   Antibody

Antigen

Antibody binds
to antigen

Bacterium

B

Complement protein

Complement protein attaches
to antibody-antigen complex
and becomes a binding site for
additional complement proteins

C

Additional complement
proteins

Additional
complement
proteins bind
to complex

D

Inflammatory mediator

One complement protein detaches
and becomes an inflammatory
mediator

E

Other complement proteins
make a hole
in the cell

© Infobase Publishing

Figure 2.4   The classical complement pathway works with antibodies
that bind to antigens on the surface of foreign cells, such as bacterial
cells. In the series of reactions that follows, fragments of the first
complement proteins are released and serve to recruit additional
complement proteins to the site of the infection. These fragments
also serve as inflammatory mediators. Eventually several different
complement proteins will bind to the foreign cell and create a hole in the
wall or membrane of that cell, resulting in its destruction.

In addition to punching holes in bacterial cells, fragments of some complement proteins act as inflammatory mediators, causing capillaries to dilate and allowing fluid and cells from the circulatory system to enter the site where the bacteria are found. Some of the fragments that stick to the bacterial cells serve to attract macrophages and activate phagocytosis.

The role of complement systems in protecting us from infection is best understood by observing people with defective complement systems. Some individuals are born with genetic defects that prevent them from making one or more of the complement proteins. These individuals are much more susceptible to certain bacterial infections and, as a result, are sick more often than people with normal complement systems. As a group, people born with defective complement systems are more likely to die from certain bacterial infections than those who have functioning complement systems.

THE CONSEQUENCE OF INNATE IMMUNITY

As you can see, the innate, or nonspecific, defenses are very important in helping us to avoid infections and to fight foreign microorganisms before they have a chance to multiply and to establish an infection. The combination of the barrier defenses and nonspecific reactive defenses is usually effective in helping us avoid infectious diseases. Unfortunately, sometimes these innate defenses are not quite enough, and infectious microorganisms make it into our bodies and begin to reproduce. The next chapter will identify some of the important cells, tissues, and organs that fight infectious microorganisms that make it past the innate defenses.

CONNECTIONS

In this chapter we have seen that the body has a number of innate, general immune defenses. The skin and mucous membranes serve as protective barriers to keep foreign organisms out of the more sensitive body areas. This defense works like the moat and defensive walls of a castle. When foreign organisms breach these defenses, the body has other general defenses. The inflammatory response is a generalized reaction to anything foreign or to cell damage. Either the foreign organism or the damaged tissues themselves send out inflammatory mediators that cause the compromised area to flood with fluids, bringing in a huge number of proteins and defensive cells to ward off the invaders.

Among the cells brought to the site are macrophages and other phagocytic cells. These cells engulf foreign microorganisms, subjecting the microbes to a series of powerful chemicals and enzymes that lead to their destruction. Finally, we learned about the complement system, a series of proteins found in blood serum that sets off a chain reaction that ultimately leads to proteins creating holes in the invading cells, allowing the influx of water that causes the cell to lyse. Like any good defense plan, the innate immune system has backup after backup to ensure that most invaders are dealt with before they can cause harm.

3

Cells, Tissues, and Organs of the Immune System

THE DIVERSITY OF THE IMMUNE SYSTEM

Unlike some of the other systems of the body, it is not easy to recognize all of the players of the immune system (Figure 3.1). Although there are three basic types of muscles, they all share certain characteristics and it is easy to see that they make up a cohesive muscular system. Likewise, although bones come in all shapes and sizes, they are more alike than they are different, and, as a result, the skeletal system is fairly easy to identify. The immune system, on the other hand, is made up of a wide variety of components. Some of these components exist as single cells. Others are specific sets of tissues, and still others are complex organs. As we will learn in this chapter, we find parts of the immune system throughout the body, and we often mistake them for parts of other body systems. In fact, in some cases the components of the immune system are integral parts of other systems of the body.

In this chapter, we will begin to identify the players in the immune system. We will not delve into their specific functions in detail here. We will see how these components function, either

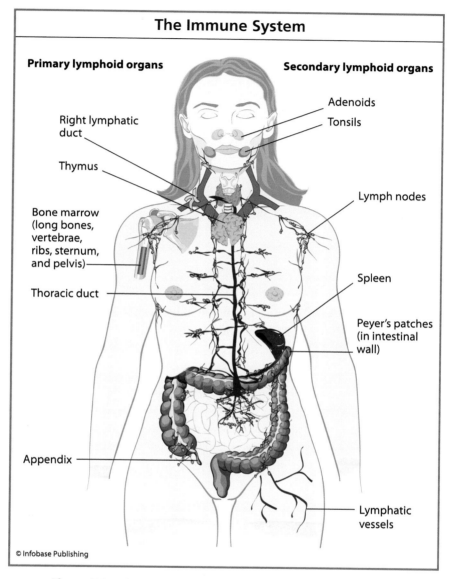

The Immune System

Primary lymphoid organs

Secondary lymphoid organs

Adenoids

Tonsils

Right lymphatic duct

Thymus

Lymph nodes

Bone marrow (long bones, vertebrae, ribs, sternum, and pelvis)

Thoracic duct

Spleen

Peyer's patches (in intestinal wall)

Appendix

Lymphatic vessels

© Infobase Publishing

Figure 3.1   The primary organs of the immune system include the bone marrow and the thymus, where immune-active cells are made or mature. The secondary organs, including the tonsils, adenoids, spleen, lymph nodes, and others, are sites where immune-active cells attack and destroy foreign materials.

Figure 3.2a Mature red blood cells are disk-shaped with depressed centers and do not contain a nucleus. White blood cells vary in appearance and do contain nuclei.

alone or together, in later chapters in the book. For the sake of convenience, we will cluster these various immune system components into four categories: individual cells, tissues, organs, and multiorgan systems. We will begin our exploration with the most basic of these classes, the individual cells.

INDIVIDUAL CELL TYPES IMPORTANT TO THE IMMUNE SYSTEM

The most important individual cells of the immune system are the many kinds of **white blood cells** (Figure 3.2a and b). Although these cells differ in appearance and function, they are all derived from the same source; in fact, all blood cells are generated by red bone marrow, the soft central core of many of the long bones of the body. Within the bone marrow are a group of special cells, called *stem cells*. These cells are

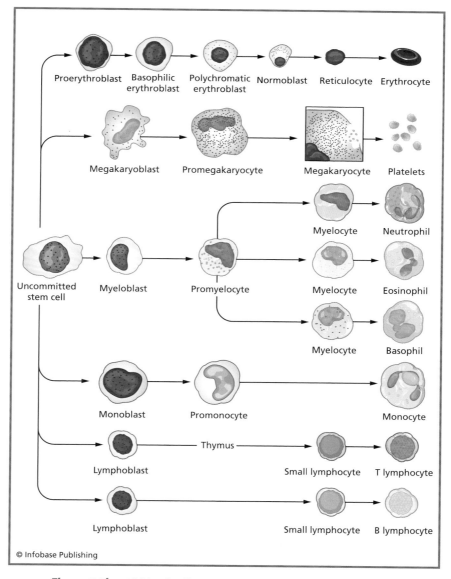

© Infobase Publishing

Figure 3.2b   All blood cells arise from uncommitted stem cells found in the marrow of long bones. Red blood cells are primarily involved in gas transport, carrying oxygen from the lungs to the tissues and carbon dioxide from the tissues to the lungs. White blood cells are much more diverse and are usually involved in the various processes of the immune system.

"undifferentiated" and can give rise to different types of cells. Once a cell differentiates, it can make additional copies of itself only when it undergoes mitosis, but an undifferentiated cell can divide and generate multiple types of cells. The process of making blood cells is called **hematopoiesis**. Hematopoiesis gives rise to **erythrocytes**, or red blood cells, which are vital in transporting oxygen and carbon dioxide throughout the body, and to **leukocytes**, or white blood cells, which are critical for the immune response. You may have also learned that platelets are a type of blood cell. Actually, platelets, which are crucial for blood clotting, are fragments of blood cells, but they too are derived from the stem cells in red bone marrow. Since our focus is on the immune system, we will dispense with further discussion of erythrocytes and platelets here and will focus on the leukocytes.

As bone marrow stem cells begin to divide, they can differentiate into a major precursor cell class called the leukocytes. Leukocytes further differentiate into two major classes: the phagocytic family and the lymphoid family. The phagocyte precursor cell can then differentiate further. Two derivatives of this cell are the mononuclear leukocytes and the polymorphonuclear leukocytes (granulated leukocytes). These long, technical names may seem a little intimidating, but if you break them down into the meanings of their root components, you will learn something about the structure of the cells. For the **mononuclear leukocytes**, "mono" means "one" and "nuclear" means "nucleus." All of these cells contain a single nucleus. These cells are also called *agranulocytes* because they do not contain granules of special proteins or chemicals in special organelles of the cytoplasm. Mononuclear leukocytes develop into **monocytes,** which make up about 8% of all leukocytes in the blood. Later, some of these monocytes can further differentiate into macrophages, cells important in fighting infection. Macrophages are not found in the bloodstream itself, but seem to develop from monocytes as the monocytes squeeze through the walls of capillaries and move into the fluids that bathe the tissues of the body.

Polymorphonuclear leukocytes are more complex than mononuclear leukocytes. *Poly* means "many," *morpho* means "shape," and *nuclear* means "nucleus." Thus, these cells have nuclei with differing shapes. Polymorphonuclear leukocytes can develop into three different types of cells. **Neutrophils** are polymorphonuclear leukocytes that have neutral granules, "neutral" meaning that they have no net charge. These cells stain poorly because most of the dyes used to stain human cells do so through charged groups on the stain surface. Because the neutrophils are electrically neutral, they do not bind stains well. The neutrophils are the largest class of polymorphonuclear leukocytes, constituting more than 50% of all leukocytes.

A second class of this family is the **eosinophils**. Eosin is a red dye that has a net negative charge; the granules of eosinophils have a net positive charge, so they bind to this dye. Eosinophil means "eosin loving." Although the eosinophils make up only a small part of the total leukocyte population in the blood (about 6%), they are very important in fighting infections caused by fungi, protozoa, and worms.

The final group of polymorphonuclear leukocytes is the **basophils**. Basophils contain granules made of compounds with a net negative charge so they bind to positively charged dyes, which are also called basic dyes. Methylene blue is one such dye, and when added to a blood smear, basophils will bind the methylene blue, taking on a blue color for their granules. The basophils are the least numerous of the leukocytes, making up less than 1% of the total leukocytes in the blood. Basophils seem to be closely related to another group of cells, called **mast cells**. Both basophils and mast cells contain a compound called *histamine*. When activated, these cells release the histamine, resulting in an inflammatory reaction. Basophils and mast cells are directly involved in allergic reactions, which is why we will often take antihistamines to fight the symptoms of allergies (stuffiness, runny nose, etc.). Antihistamines block the action of histamine.

The second major family of leukocytes derived from bone marrow stem cells is the **lymphoid family**. Depending on where in the body these cells mature, they develop into one of two cell types. When the lymphoid precursor cell remains in the bone marrow to mature, it becomes a **B lymphocyte**, or **B cell**. B cells are the principal cells for making antibodies. We will discuss this process in chapters 4 and 5. When the lymphoid precursor cells migrate to the thymus, a gland that lies in front of the heart, the precursors become one of a number of types of **T lymphocytes**, or **T cells**. T cells mediate a process known as **cell-mediated immunity**. They are also critical in regulating the intensity of the immune reaction. There are three major divisions of T cells. **Cytotoxic T cells** (T_C cells) carry out cell-mediated immunity. T-helper cells (T_H cells) are central in activating immune responses, and **suppressor T cells** (T_S cells) reduce the intensity of the immune system and also probably play an important role in helping our bodies distinguish our own tissues and cells from those of invading materials.

A third class of lymphoid cells that is less well understood is the non-B, non-T, or **null lymphocytes**. These cells can be distinguished from B and T cells by the absence of certain surface structures. They tend to fight infections, but do so nonspecifically, whereas B cells and cytotoxic T cells are programmed to attack very specific foreign antigens.

TISSUES OF THE IMMUNE SYSTEM

In addition to the cells that directly fight infection or regulate the immune process, there are also clusters of cells that form tissues critical for immunity. The tonsils are a ring of lymphoid tissue located at the back of the mouth, just at the top of the throat. Your doctor or nurse will "swab" the tonsils with a sterile applicator when he or she is checking for strep throat. Closely related tissues found in the nose are the adenoids. These patches of tissue are positioned where the nasal area opens into the throat. The tonsils and the adenoids are rich in all types of leukocytes. When a foreign organism enters the body through the mouth or nose, it is usually transported to either the tonsils or the adenoids where the cells of the immune system launch an attack. We have learned only in recent years the important role that these tissues play in preventing infections that enter through the respiratory system. Now that we know the critical role the tonsils and the adenoids play in fighting infection, doctors are much more hesitant to remove them.

Another important mass of lymphoid tissue is the appendix. As with the tonsils, it was much more common to remove a person's appendix a generation or two ago because we did not know its function. We assumed that it was unessential and therefore if it became inflamed (which would not be unusual for a lymphoid tissue), we thought it could be removed with no ill effects. Although we still do not completely understand the role of the appendix, it is probably important in protecting the lower digestive tract and the body cavity from infectious agents that enter the body in food or water.

The final general group of lymphoid tissues is the **Peyer's patches**. Peyer's patches are small pockets of lymphoid tissue found in the intestines. They may play a protective role similar to that of the appendix. Closely related to Peyer's patches are **skin-associated lymphoid tissue (SALT)** and **mucosa-associated lymphoid tissue (MALT).** These patches of tissue are located below the surface of the skin and mucous membranes, respectively. They are critical in preventing infections caused by infectious organisms that cross these natural barriers. The importance of SALT has been demonstrated in burn patients. Severe burn patients whose SALT patches are intact and functional are much less likely to have their burns become infected than are those whose SALT patches are damaged by the burn.

ORGANS OF THE IMMUNE SYSTEM

An organ is a collection of different tissues that work together to perform one or more important functions. The organs of the immune system can be divided into two major classes. Primary lymphoid organs include the bone marrow and the thymus. They are essential for the production and development of the various classes of lymphocytes. Bone marrow is the site of blood cell production, including lymphocytes. The bones most important in this process are the vertebrae, the ribs, the sternum, the long bones of the arms and legs, and the pelvis. Bone marrow not only gives rise to all types of blood cells, but it is also the location for the specialization of B cells. The second primary lymphoid organ is the thymus. As mentioned previously, the thymus is a small organ located just in front of the heart. The thymus is critical in the development and maturation of T cells.

The secondary lymphoid organs are the lymph nodes (Figure 3.3) and the spleen. **Lymph** is fluid that is forced out of the blood vessels and bathes the body tissues directly. It is returned to the circulatory system by a system of lymph vessels that arise in the body tissues and eventually dump the lymph into a vein near the heart. Lymph transports many of the important components of the immune system. Before the lymph is returned to the circulatory system, it passes through masses of lymphoid tissue called lymph nodes. Collectively, the lymph, lymph vessels, and lymph nodes make up the **lymphatic system.**

Have you ever noticed that sometimes when you have a sore throat, the "glands" in your neck get swollen? Those glands are actually lymph nodes that are fighting infection. Because they activate the immune system within their structure, the tissues of the lymph nodes become inflamed and sore. Lymph nodes are scattered throughout the body, but especially along the neck and trunk. There are significant concentrations of lymph nodes in the area of the hip joint, along the abdomen, under the sternum and around

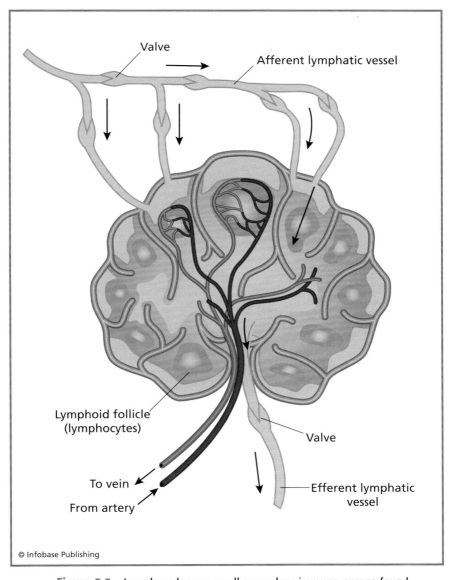

Valve

Afferent lymphatic vessel

Lymphoid follicle
(lymphocytes)

Valve

To vein

From artery

Efferent lymphatic
vessel

© Infobase Publishing

Figure 3.3   Lymph nodes are small secondary immune organs found at the intersections of lymphatic vessels. These nodes attract and retain phagocytic cells and other immune-active cells. They are often sites where infecting bacteria are attacked. In certain infections, the lymph nodes become so inflamed they swell and become extremely painful. Lymph nodes also capture cancer cells that are released from tumors.

the breasts, and under the arms and into the neck. The word "node" means a point of connection. The lymph nodes are the locations where various branches of the lymphatic system come together. We will discuss the lymphatic system in the final section of this chapter.

In addition to the lymph nodes, the spleen is another very important secondary lymphatic organ. The spleen is located in the upper part of the abdomen, just below the diaphragm. The spleen is fed by a large number of blood vessels, and, as a result, the blood spends a significant amount of time in the spleen. Unfortunately, the spleen is not very well protected by the body. It is not unusual when a person has a serious blow to the abdomen, as one might experience in a serious automobile accident, a fall, or a crushing blow, for the spleen to rupture. Because so much blood flows through the spleen, a rupture of the spleen can cause massive internal bleeding, and, as a result, it may have to be removed to prevent the victim from bleeding to death. Fortunately, this is fairly routine surgery, and most patients recover from a splenectomy. Unfortunately, without a spleen, these individuals typically suffer from many more infections than persons with a functional spleen, indicating the importance of this organ in immune defense.

LYMPHATIC CIRCULATION

We tend to think of the circulatory system as a closed loop of tubes—arteries, capillaries, and veins—that transport blood from the heart to the lungs and to the body. However, the circulatory system is not completely closed. The blood is under pressure, and this pressure forces some of the fluid of the blood, the plasma, through the walls of blood vessels, mainly the capillaries. Once the fluid leaves the circulatory system and enters the tissues, it is referred to as *lymph*. Obviously, if fluid leaks out of the circulatory system and gets out into the tissues, there has to be a way to return it to the bloodstream. The fluids around the tissues drain into tiny tubes called lymphatic vessels. These lymphatic vessels merge into larger vessels at intersections marked by lymph nodes. Ultimately, all of the lymphatic vessels and lymph nodes merge into the final components of lymphatic circulation, the thoracic duct and right lymphatic duct. These ducts empty the lymph from the lymphatic system into large veins near the heart, thus returning the fluid to the circulatory system.

Additionally, monocytes, one of the classes of white blood cells, can also squeeze through the walls of the capillaries when signaled to do so. When they do, these cells undergo another transformation and become macrophages. Macrophages are large polymorphonuclear leukocytes that wander around the tissues looking for foreign invaders. When they find them, they engulf the proteins, bacteria, viruses, or whatever these foreign invaders happen to be and destroy them. Moreover, they will actually use pieces of these destroyed materials to activate the immune system to fight even harder.

CONNECTIONS

The immune system is a very complicated and essential system of the human body. It involves the action of individual cells, specific tissues and organs, and a fluid-filled system of vessels that is separate from, but linked to, the circulatory system. In later chapters, we will explore some of the specific ways that the various parts of the immune system work together to protect the body from infections and sometimes from its own cells.

4

Humoral Immunity

THE BASIC UNIT OF HUMORAL IMMUNITY: THE ANTIBODY

The **humoral immune system** IS A POWERFUL DEFENSE AGAINST foreign materials (bacteria, viruses, fungi, toxins, etc.) that make it past the barrier defenses and enter into the deeper tissues or the bloodstream. The basic functional units of humoral immunity are special molecules called **antibodies,** also called **immunoglobulins (Ig)**. The molecules attacked by antibodies are called **antigens.** Antibodies bind to antigens, acting as "tags" that label the antigens. These tags trigger processes that inactivate or destroy the antigens.

Antibodies are made of proteins that are joined together in very specific configurations. The body has five basic types of antibodies. The first is *immunoglobulin G (IgG)*, the most common antibody type in the blood. The second most common type is *immunoglobulin M (IgM)*, a very large complex that contains five IgG-like molecules joined together in a huge complex. IgM is the form of antibody produced the first time the immune system is exposed to a new foreign agent. *Immunoglobulin A (IgA)* is an antibody type made of two IgG-like complexes joined together. As long as these two units remain joined together, the IgA molecule can be secreted across the mucous membranes. For this reason, IgA is very important in defending us from infections in areas with lots of membranes. IgA, for instance, is secreted across the mucous membranes of the respiratory system to fight infections of the nose and throat. It also is secreted across the lining of the intestinal tract to defend us from infections of the digestive system.

Immunoglobulin E (IgE) is a special class of antibody. It is found only in low concentrations and helps to fight parasitic infections (infections by fungi, worms, and protozoa). IgE is shaped like IgG, but has a constant end of the molecule that binds granular white blood cells and mast cells. When these cells bind an IgE molecule that has bound an antigen, the granular white blood cells and mast cells degranulate—that is, they release their contents. Among these contents are histamine and other inflammatory mediators that trigger inflammation.

If you have hay fever, your body makes IgE against certain types of pollen. If you inhale that pollen into the mouth and nose, IgE will bind the pollen antigens, trigger binding of the IgE molecule to the mast cells and granular white blood cells, and will cause histamine release. This causes the tissues in your nose to become inflamed. The swelling of the tissues makes your nose feel "stuffy" and causes fluid to drain, giving you a runny nose.

The last type of antibody is *immunoglobulin D (IgD)*. IgD is found on the surface of B cells and T cells and serves as the antigen receptor site that triggers cell activation and immune response.

ANTIBODY STRUCTURE

The IgG molecule is made up of four proteins. There are two identical large proteins and two identical smaller proteins. These proteins join together to form a "Y"-shaped molecule (Figure 4.1). The two large proteins form the basic structure of the Y. They are joined together by chemical bonds in the base of the Y. The ends of the large molecules that make the base

Figure 4.1 Antibodies, or immunoglobulins, are proteins made by B cells. Different B cells produce different IgG molecules. Immunoglobulin G (IgG) is made up of two large proteins (the heavy chains) and two small proteins (the light chains). These proteins join together to form a Y-shaped molecule. The "arms" of the Y, the variable regions, are identical, allowing each IgG to bind two identical antigens. The constant region of IgG is always the same, even when antibodies are made by different B cells, but the variable regions are unique for each B cell and will only bind one specific antigen.

are called constant regions. That is, all human IgG molecules have exactly the same amino acids making up this stem, regardless of which antigen binds to that particular antibody. These constant regions continue about halfway up each arm of the Y. Small proteins line the inside of the arms of the Y, and each is joined by chemical bonds to the upper end of a large protein molecule. As a result, all four proteins are physically bonded to each other and cannot come apart. The half of the small protein molecules toward the base are constant for all IgG molecules. The upper ends of the large and the small proteins that make the tips of the arms are called variable regions. It is these variable regions that make the antibodies specific for binding a given antigen. The shape and charges (positive or negative) of the variable regions determine which antigen the antibody molecule will bind. Because the two upper arms are identical, each IgG molecule has the ability to bind two identical antigens. The same is true for IgE and IgD antibodies—each will bind two identical antigens. Because IgM is made up of five basic subunits and because each binds two antigens, the IgM molecules can bind ten identical antigens at once. IgA is a dimer, made up of two identical antibody units so each IgA molecule can bind four antigens.

The variable regions of the antibodies make them specific for one particular antigen. The constant regions are also important because they are recognized by different components of the immune system. Interestingly, while every IgG molecule in a human has the same constant regions, regardless of the antigens that it binds, the IgG constant region of a human is different from that of a mouse, or a horse, or a rabbit. Every animal species that makes antibodies has its own unique constant region.

Later we will look at an example of how antibodies are made in response to a bacterial infection. Most foreign cells have many copies of their antigens on their surfaces, perhaps hundreds of copies of those surface antigens. Because each cell has lots of antigens, and each IgG molecule has two antigen binding sites, IgG molecules tend to bind to the surface of bacterial cells by turning the Y upside down (Figure 4.2). The arms of the Y attach to the cell, each arm to a different copy of the same antigen. When there are multiple bacterial cells present, as there almost always are in an infection (there may be thousands or millions of identical bacterial cells), some of the IgG molecules will join two bacterial cells together—that is, one arm of the IgG will bind to an antigen on one cell while the other binds to an identical antigen of another cell. The result is that the antibodies tend to clump the foreign cells together. This clumping concentrates the foreign bacteria into clusters that can be more easily targeted by the immune system.

Recall that IgM has ten antigen binding sites and that we said it is the type of antibody made on first exposure to a particular foreign antigen. When the body is first exposed to the antigen, the humoral immune system takes about ten days before it is fully up to strength. If the foreign antigen is on a bacterial cell, these cells will be constantly reproducing during those ten days. By the time your immune system can strike back, the numbers of bacteria are very large. Because each IgM can bind ten antigens, these antibody molecules tend to quickly tie up the bacteria into large clumps. This helps our bodies to fight back, but often not before the bacterium (or virus or other agent) has made us sick. When we are exposed to the same microorganism later, the immune system can respond much more quickly, usually in a matter of two to three days. This usually eliminates the microbes before they cause damage and disease, which is the reason why we get only certain diseases, such as measles and mumps, once. Any time we are exposed to the same virus after the first exposure, the immune system responds very quickly and produces lots of IgG antibody. This allows us to fight off the virus before the disease can occur again.

A BIOLOGICAL MYSTERY SOLVED

When scientists first began to understand how the immune system worked, they were faced with a difficult question. They

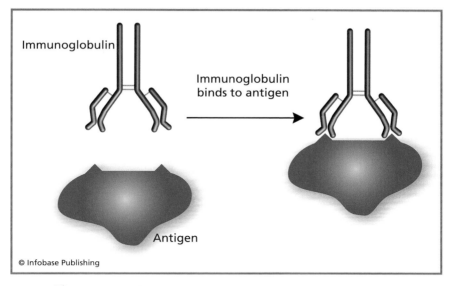

Figure 4.2   Each IgG molecule has two antigen binding sites. Typically, bacteria and other infectious organisms will have multiple copies of key antigens on their surface. When an IgG molecule binds to two of these identical surface antigens on two identical bacterial cells, large complexes of antigens and antibodies will form. Note that the antibody binds to the surface of the bacterial cell by attaching the variable regions to the surface antigens. This turns the Y-shaped molecule upside down so that the constant regions are then available to recruit the complement system or other immune-active cells.

knew from molecular biology that every protein in the body has its own gene. When it became clear that immunoglobulins could be made that can specifically bind to literally thousands of different antigens, molecular biologists wanted to know where all these different genes were stored. There was not enough room on the human chromosomes to accommodate all these different immunoglobulin genes. The idea that the body could make different proteins without having a gene for each protein defied our basic understanding of genetics. How could this be?

When scientists began to isolate and sequence immuno-globulins (determine the specific bases that make the genes), they made an amazing discovery. In the undifferentiated B cells (those that had just been made from bone marrow stem cells and were not dedicated to make a specific antibody), there were clusters of gene sequences that were interchangeable. The typical immunoglobulin molecule could be divided into three or four distinct sections. Before the B cells differentiated, they had several alternative blocks of DNA for each of these sections of the immunoglobulin gene. These blocks were called "cassettes." To make one complete antibody gene, one cassette was needed for each section of the molecule. By rearranging different cassettes into each of the slots, you could literally get thousands of combinations. This idea may be hard to imagine. Let's think about using a more concrete model.

Suppose you have an entertainment center on which you can play cassette tapes, DVDs, CDs, and computer games. Now let's assume that you have four sets of earphones and you can run the four devices all at the same time so that four of your friends can use the entertainment center at once. In your collection of media, you have 30 cassette tapes, 45 CDs, 20 DVDs, and 15 computer games. How many different combinations of things can your friends enjoy at any one time? You can determine the number of combinations by multiplying the numbers of each type of media together—30 cassette tapes, multiplied by 45 CDs, multiplied by 20 DVDs, multiplied by 15 computer games (30 x 45 x 20 x 15) equals 405,000 different combinations!

Now let's take a simple four-cassette model for an antibody gene. If we assume that there are about 15 options for the first cassette position, 20 cassette options for the second, 8 cassettes for the third position, and 6 cassettes for the fourth position (15 x 20 x 8 x 6), mixing and matching these cassettes of DNA can make over 14,000 different antibody genes! Suddenly, instead of needing enough room on the chromosome for 14,000 different proteins (and therefore 14,000 different genes), we can accomplish the same number of antibody combinations with enough DNA to encode only 49 (15 + 20 + 8 + 6) cassettes, and because each cassette is only a small part of a gene, very little room on the chromosomes of the human genome is required.

A ONE-TIME EVENT

Measles, mumps, German measles, and chickenpox, once common childhood diseases, are rarely seen in the United States these days. In fact, most young Americans will probably never suffer from these diseases. However, things were very different for your parents and grandparents. Most Americans the ages of your parents or grandparents have had at least one, or in many cases, all of these diseases.

Why did your parents and grandparents have these diseases and you probably did not? Normally our bodies do not produce antibodies against a microorganism unless we are exposed to that microbe. Your parents and grandparents would have been exposed to these diseases and the microbes (all viruses) that caused them. Although these diseases are still very common and are the cause of many deaths and permanent disabilities in other parts of the world, they are very rare in the United States because the United States began an aggressive program of vaccination against childhood diseases about 50 years ago. A **vaccination** is exposure to a form of the virus or a part of the virus that is incapable of causing the full symptoms of the disease, but is enough like the viruses to "trick" the body into thinking it has been exposed to these viruses. Most American children receive vaccines for these diseases when they are quite young. The chickenpox vaccine, however, was just recently developed (this may explain why you had chickenpox, but not the other three diseases). These vaccines are required for all children entering school. As a result, virtually no young person in the United States is likely to experience these diseases in the future as long as regular vaccination continues. The vaccines activate the cells that make antibodies against each of the viruses so that the body has a significant number of these antibodies against each virus. When the body is exposed to the viruses, the antibodies direct the immune system to destroy them before the virus can cause disease.

The only problem with this model is that once a cell is programmed to make a particular antibody, what prevents it from rearranging cassettes? When a B cell matures in the bone marrow, it randomly creates one unique arrangement of four cassettes. Once this is done, it becomes a permanent gene for that B cell, and all the other cassettes are lost. Thus, that B cell and all the cloned B cells that are made from it will be able to produce only one type of antibody that will recognize only one possible antigen. Since the processes of selecting the cassettes is random in the undifferentiated precursor B cell (the B cell that has not yet programmed a cassette combination), literally thousands of different specialized B cells are made in the bone marrow and are then "programmed" to each have only one option for antibody production.

CONNECTIONS

In this chapter, we have learned about the most important functioning molecules of the humoral immune system: antibodies, or immunoglobulins. There are five different types of immunoglobulins in the human body, and each has its own function. We have also learned how antibodies bind to antigens and why the constant regions of the antibodies are important. Finally, we have learned the "trick" that our genes have played to give us thousands of different antibodies without having to have thousands of different genes to encode them. What we have not learned is how we trigger the B cells to make and secrete antibodies. We will explore this topic in the next chapter.

5

Antibody Synthesis

HOW AND WHEN ARE ANTIBODIES MADE?

RECALL FROM THE PREVIOUS CHAPTERS THAT THERE ARE two classes of lymphocytes important in immunity. The B lymphocytes, or B cells, are most important in the humoral immunity. In addition, certain T lymphocytes and phagocytic cells are also important in antibody production. Recall that B cells are produced from bone marrow stem cells and that they remain in the bone marrow where they specialize and develop. During this development phase, each B cell is programmed to produce only one specific type of antibody. This antibody is unique and will bind only to one antigen. This binding is very specific, like a hand in a custom-made glove. Once the B cell specializes and matures, its outer surface becomes coated with IgD molecules that serve as antigen receptors or binding sites. These antigen receptors are critical for activation of the B cell and, therefore, for the production of antibodies.

Any large biological molecule can activate the immune system. These molecules are often proteins, but **polysaccharides**, which are complexes of sugars and nucleic acids, can also activate the humoral immune system. Because viruses and microbial cells actually contain many different antigens on their surfaces, more than one type of antibody can bind to these cells. The first step in the humoral immune reaction is activation (Figure 5.1). Activation requires antigens, but the antigens have to be attached to fairly big molecules. It is possible to have a biomolecule that is an antigen (an antigenic molecule) but which is too small to start the series of reactions needed for humoral response. Antigens that are big enough to start this process are called **immunogens**, which means "immune starting." Smaller antigens can be attached to another large complex molecule, and they, too, can become immunogenic. Although there are many ways for the humoral immune system to be activated, we will look at only one example. We will explore what happens to the humoral immune system when it is exposed to a foreign bacterial cell. The same principles apply for viruses and for other microorganisms.

A GERM INVADES: FIRST EXPOSURE ACTIVATION

Let us look at an example in which a bacterium makes it past the innate immune system and enters the deeper tissues (see Figure 5.1 for an explanation of the different immune pathways). We will also assume that this is the first time this particular disease-causing bacterium has made it into the parts of the body protected by the acquired immune system. This might occur when you get cut on a dirty object or when your natural defenses are down and the bacterium makes it through the physical lines of defense. You will recall that there are phagocytic cells, macrophages that are part of the nonspecific immune system. They recognize that the bacterium is foreign to the body, and they bind and engulf the bacterial cell.

Remember that once inside the macrophage, the enzymes and chemicals contained in vacuoles in the macrophage begin to attack the bacterium, breaking it down into little pieces. Once the bacterium is destroyed, the macrophage places the antigen-containing pieces of the bacterium on the macrophage cell surface at special sites called antigen-presenting sites.

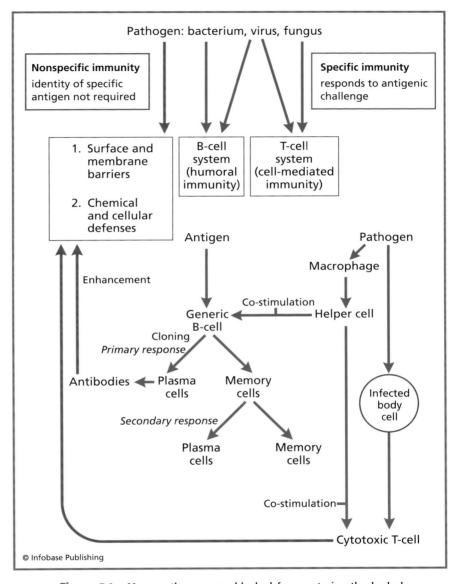

Figure 5.1 Many pathogens are blocked from entering the body by the skin and mucous membranes and by the chemical defenses that constitute nonspecific immunity. When a pathogen breaches these defenses, the actions of the humoral immune system (B-cell mediated) and the cell-mediated immune system (T-cell mediated) attack it.

As soon as these fragments of the bacterial cell are in place, the macrophage sends out chemical messages to attract a special group of lymphocytes called T-helper cells. The T-helper cells (T_H cells) are attracted to the macrophage by these chemical messages. T_H cells have special sites on their surface called CD4 receptors. These receptors bind very tightly to the antigen-presenting site on the macrophage, but only if it is presenting an antigen. Once these T-helper cells are bound to the macrophage, they are close enough to receive chemical messages from it. Leukocytes, both lymphoid cells like B cells and T cells and nonlymphoid cells like macrophages, produce and release a host of different chemical messages called **interleukins**. Interleukin literally means "between leukocytes" and reflects the fact that these molecules transmit messages from one type of leukocyte to another. The messages change the behavior of the second cell. It can cause it to move toward the first cell as we saw for the first messenger molecule from the macrophage, or it can change the activity of the second cell in other ways. When the two cells are held together by binding of the CD4 receptor to the antigen-presenting site, a different interleukin is released from the macrophage that causes the T-helper cell to produce and secrete its own interleukin messenger molecules.

The interleukin produced by the T-helper cell also serves as an attractant, but in this case, it recruits B lymphocytes (B cells) to the macrophage/T-helper complex. This interleukin attracts all B cells, regardless of the antibodies they produce. Most B cells will float into the area with the other two cells, but because they do not recognize an antigen on the macrophage antigen-presenting complex, they will drift away. B cells that have IgD molecules on their surface that bind the antigen presented by the macrophage are attracted to the complex and bind to it. These B cells become tightly associated with the macrophage/T-helper cell complex and remain at the site.

Once the B cell is in place, the T-helper cell releases yet another interleukin. This interleukin molecule stimulates the

B cell to reproduce. Why is this important? Remember that B cells make only one type of antibody. Until exposed to an antigen, the body will keep only a very limited number of each B cell (probably fewer than than 10) for any given antigen. We have assumed in this activation example that there was only one bacterial cell, but more likely, there will be hundreds or thousands of these bacterial cells. It will take more antibodies than 10 B cells could produce to fight off the possible infection.

B CELL ACTIVATION

Once the B cell has been recruited to the complex by the interleukin released from the T-helper cell, it is said to be "activated." The B cell will reproduce by mitosis (cell division), making many new identical B cells that produce the same antibodies. Because only B cells with IgD receptors that match the antigens on the macrophage-presenting site are activated, all of the B cells that are produced by activation are programmed to make antibodies that will bind the presented antigen. This process is known as **B cell amplification** (Figure 5.2), and it ensures that the body only amplifies the B cells needed to attack the invading bacteria. As the B cells reproduce, they differentiate into two cell types: **plasma cells** and **memory cells**. Plasma cells are very large cells that are dedicated factories for producing and secreting (releasing) antibody molecules. They make thousands of identical antibody molecules that are secreted into the bloodstream or into the lymphatic fluid that bathes the tissues. These antibodies are mostly IgM antibodies and, as a result, have multiple sites that can bind to antigens. Because viruses or bacterial cells have lots of antigens on their surfaces, the antibodies and antigen-covered cells form complexes. As these complexes form, the B cells release their own interleukins that attract phagocytic cells and complement proteins, eventually leading to the elimination of the bacterial cells.

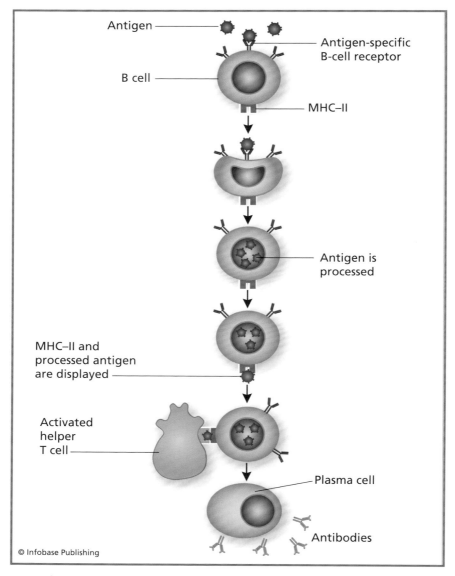

Figure 5.2 Foreign antigens bind to specific receptors on B cells programmed to produce antibodies against that specific antigen. Once bound to the B cell surface, the antigen is internalized and processed. Portions of the antigen are presented on the surface of the B cell at MHC-II sites. When these sites are occupied by the processed antigen they recruit T helper cells which release chemical signals that cause the B cell to become activated, making new plasma cells and memory B cells.

Memory cells, the other class of differentiated B cells, are almost identical to the first B cell that was activated, but there are many more memory cells for a given antigen than there were of the unamplified B cells. The memory cells do not produce or secrete antibodies, but they remain in the body. If the antigen is seen again at a later time, these cells can be quickly activated for antibody production.

The process of activating the original B cells, producing plasma cells and memory B cells, and producing enough antibody molecules from the plasma cells to tie up all the bacterial cells and to allow the immune system to get rid of those cells takes about 7 to 10 days. Because the bacteria (or viruses) are reproducing all this time, they will often overwhelm the body and will result in disease symptoms. As we will see in the next section, future exposures activate the memory B cells much more quickly, usually within two to four days. Because the body mounts the humoral response quickly, it tends to eliminate the microbes before they can cause enough damage to result in disease symptoms.

FIRST EXPOSURE USING VACCINES

It is possible to get the protection of an activated humoral immune system without suffering from a disease. In the last chapter we spoke of the MMR and the chickenpox vaccines and how these vaccines prevent many people from contracting these diseases. Vaccines are made either from microbes that are chemically altered so that they cannot grow or modified so that they cause only very mild symptoms, or they may consist of only one or two of the antigens, not the entire microbial cell. When we are vaccinated, the antigens that are introduced in the injection make the body think it has been infected by the microbe because some of the microbial antigens are present. These antigens activate the immune system just as the infectious bacterium or virus does, but because the vaccine cannot cause disease, we get the benefit of B cell amplification and activation without becoming sick. Once the body has produced plasma cells and memory cells that respond to that antigen, the memory cells are already amplified and ready to respond if the microbe enters the body. The next section indicates what happens when the body is challenged by a microbe after an initial exposure.

ACTIVATION OF HUMORAL IMMUNITY— SECONDARY RESPONSE

Once a B cell line has been activated and plasma and memory cells are generated from it, any future exposure to the same antigen (either the second exposure or the seventy-second one) is considered a "secondary" response. This is because every exposure after the first is just like every other subsequent exposure.

THE WORLD OF COCA-COLA

Coca-Cola is a worldwide corporation, and its signature drink, Coca-Cola, has become an international business icon. Travel to almost any city in the world and you will find products from the Coca-Cola Company. International headquarters for this multinational corporation is based in Atlanta, Georgia. If you are visiting downtown Atlanta, you might consider a visit to The World of Coca-Cola, an interactive museum for the world's most popular soft drink. By far, the most popular stop on the tour is the tasting room. In addition to the company's very familiar drinks—Coca-Cola, Sprite, and Diet Coke—the company makes dozens of other flavors. Some are very common around the world. Fanta, the company's fruit-flavored drinks, has some flavors, such as orange and grape, which are extremely popular and can be found in most parts of the world. Other flavors—tangerine, pineapple, and grapefruit, for instance—tend to be very popular in some cities, but not in others. These drinks are needed only in certain countries; consequently, the company produces them in only a limited number of its production facilities.

Perhaps one of the most regional flavors for Coca-Cola is Beverly. Beverly is flavored with bitters. Interestingly, bitters are very popular drinks in Italy. The Coca-Cola Company produces a lot

Once memory cells are in place for a specific antigen, if the body is exposed to that antigen, the process of activation occurs just as it did on first exposure. If the antigen is on a bacterial cell, a macrophage will engulf and break down the cell into small pieces. Antigens from the cell are presented on the antigen-presenting sites on the surface of the macrophage. T-helper cells are recruited; these cells, in turn, recruit memory B cells. When memory B cells enter the complex and bind to the antigen on the macrophage, these cells become activated and reproduce, making more plasma cells and additional memory B cells. Since there are so many more memory B cells for the antigen than there were inactivated B cells at the first (primary) exposure, the memory B cells activate much more

of Beverly at its facilities in Italy and virtually nowhere else. Some flavors of drinks change in popularity. Before the formulation of Diet Coke, another diet drink made by Coca-Cola, Tab, was very popular and was made in many of its plants. With the formulation of Diet Coke, the popularity of Tab has declined on a global scale. As a result, Coca-Cola has reduced the number of plants that make Tab, leaving it in production only where there is still a demand.

Our B cells can be viewed as different factories for different products. Just as the Coca-Cola Company makes different products on different manufacturing lines at different plants, our bodies make different antibodies from different B cells. As market demand for Coca-Cola products increases, the number of plants making the product also increases, and as the demand decreases, plants are closed or redirected so that they do not produce more of a flavor than the company can market. Our bodies regulate antibody production in much the same way. As the number of molecules of a particular antigen increases, the body will increase the number of B cells that make an antibody to attack that antigen. As the number of molecules of that antigen decreases, the number of B cells making the appropriate antibody also decreases. Our bodies monitor the "market" for particular antibodies and control production to meet the demand.

quickly, and large amounts of antibody are produced by the new plasma cells in less than half the time required for the primary exposure.

However, the plasma cells made from memory B cells are reprogrammed to produce IgG antibodies rather than the IgM antibodies synthesized by the plasma cells produced from the initial B cells. Huge amounts of antibodies are released in the first few days, and the body destroys the microbe before it can cause the damage to the body that would result in symptoms of disease.

CONNECTIONS

In this chapter we have learned how the body amplifies the B cells it needs to respond to a particular antigen. We have learned how plasma cells make and secrete antibodies and how memory cells are stored, waiting for future exposures to the same microbe. We have also learned why a first exposure often results in disease but future exposures do not, and how vaccines make it possible to avoid disease symptoms by making the body think it has seen a particular microbe before. Antibodies are very important in defending us from infection. However, there is another type of immunity, cell-mediated immunity, which functions very differently from humoral immunity but is also important, especially in fighting some viral infections and certain rare types of cancer. The next chapter will discuss the importance of the cellular immune system and how it is controlled.

6

Cell-Mediated
Immunity

T CELL TYPES

IN THE PREVIOUS TWO CHAPTERS WE HAVE FOCUSED OUR
attention on B lymphocytes, or B cells. T lymphocytes are
closely related to B cells; however, these cell precursors, generated from bone marrow stem cells, migrate to the thymus,
a patch of fatty tissue located near the heart. The thymus in
newborn children is a more developed structure, but it atro-
phies (begins to break down) as we approach adulthood. T cells
are programmed in a manner somewhat like the programming
of B cells in bone marrow. There are several different kinds of
T cells, including T-helper cells and cytotoxic T cells.

We have already discussed T-helper cells (T_H cells). These
are the cells that have CD4 receptors on their surfaces, allowing
them to bind to macrophages and other phagocytic cells that
are presenting foreign antigens. Recall that the CD4 receptor
on the T-helper cell binds to the antigen-presenting complex
on the surface of a macrophage that has engulfed a foreign particle and which is presenting antigens from that particle at the
antigen-presenting site. This complex is called the **major histocompatability complex** II (MHC-II). MHC-II is found only on
the surface of phagocytic cells; thus, only cells directly involved

in removing foreign materials can bind the CD4 receptor on the T-helper cell and thereby amplify the humoral immune response by recruiting and activating specific B cells.

All mammalian cells contain a second major histocompatability complex, MHC-I. These MHCs are unique for each species, and, in fact, there can be different variants of MHC-I in different organisms of the same species (just as we can have different hair or eye color, blood type, etc.). These MHC-I proteins help us to recognize our own cells. If you are given a blood transfusion from a person with a different blood type, or if you receive transplanted organs from someone with a different MHC-I factor, the immune system attacks the blood cells or the organ, leading to rejection and major system failure in the body.

The second class of T cells, the cytotoxic T cells (T_C cells) are very important in fighting viral and certain bacterial infections, and they help to control certain rare forms of cancer. Cytotoxic T cells have CD8 receptors on their surfaces. These receptors bind to MHC-I on the surfaces of our own cells when those cells are presenting a foreign antigen. Why are the antigens on the surface of our cells? Viruses must infect specific host cells to reproduce. Many bacteria have developed mechanisms for penetrating human cells as a way to "hide" from the humoral immune system. When a cell becomes infected by a virus or bacterium, it will present some of the antigens of that bacterium or virus on its surface at the MHC-I site.

If the infected cells are not removed, they will burst, releasing lots of new viruses or bacteria. These organisms can then go on to infect more cells. For certain forms of cancer, cancer-producing cells make new proteins that are different from normal host proteins. These different proteins can also be presented on the cell surface. In the case of cancer cells, if they are allowed to grow without restriction, they will crowd out other cells, produce tumors, and lead to death. In short, infected human cells or cancer cells present a risk to the organism as a whole. They must be eliminated before they destroy the host.

When these cells present foreign antigens at the MHC-I site, cytotoxic T cells that are specialized for that antigen respond. (Cytotoxic T cells, like B cells, are programmed for a specific antigen.) The CD8 receptor on the cytotoxic T cell binds to the MHC-I site and the IgD molecules on the surface of the cytotoxic T cell stabilize the complex by binding to the antigen. The T cells are then activated. T-helper cells are also critical to the activation of cell-mediated immunity. They join the complex of the infected or cancerous cell and the cytotoxic T cell. An interleukin is produced that stimulates the T-helper.

KILLERS FOR HIRE

Spy movies have become a staple for Hollywood. One of the more common elements in the spy movie formula is the hired assassin, or hired gun. These people learn everything they can about their targets so that they kill the right person and not someone else by mistake. Typically, they are provided with detailed information so specific that the killers can distinguish their intended targets from everyone else. Profiles of hired killers might include that they can specifically identify their targets, be prepared with the necessary weapons to do the job, and fade back into obscurity so they cannot be identified once the job is finished.

The parts of the immune system involved in cell-mediated immunity are, in many ways, like hired killers. They are programmed to kill their targets, and they can distinguish their target cells from all the other cells in the body. The immune cells carry powerful weapons with them to eliminate their targets, and once their job is done, they tend to disappear back into the bloodstream. Interestingly, the targets of the cell-mediated immune system are often our own cells. You might wonder about the logic of programming cells to destroy our own cells. The cell-mediated immune system usually attacks only those cells that present a danger to the rest of the body. The cell-mediated immune system has developed to identify body cells that have become cancerous or are infected with viruses.

The T-helper cell, in turn, produces and secretes a different interleukin that activates the cytotoxic T cells in the complex. The first response of the T_C cell is to reproduce, just as we saw for activated B cells. When the number of cytotoxic T cells is high enough, they begin their attack.

T CELL RESPONSE AGAINST VIRUSES

When human cells are infected with a virus, they respond by breaking down certain cellular proteins that bind the virus and take its antigens to the MHC-I site on the surface (Figure 6.2). At this point, the infected cell is said to be "marked." The cytotoxic T cell uses the presented antigen and the CD8/MHC-I complex to bind to the surface of the infected cell. The T cell remains attached for about 10 minutes. During this time, the T cell secretes a specialized class of proteins called **perforins**. The perforins penetrate into the membrane of the infected cell, associating with other perforins, ultimately producing a hole called a porin. These porins allow water to rush in from the outside of the cell, causing it to swell and eventually to burst. Thus, by killing the infected cell before the virus can finish replicating, the body breaks the chain of viral infection, protecting the remaining cells of the body. This process continues until all infected cells are killed.

A similar process eliminates certain forms of cancer cells. The cancer cells are recognized as foreign and are attacked by cytotoxic T cells. Perforins are then used to puncture and lyse the cancer cell. Cancer cells are also eliminated by macrophages (Figure 6.1).

Finally, bacterial cells can infect host cells, especially macrophages. Some bacteria, including the species that causes tuberculosis, actually "trick" the macrophage into engulfing the bacterium. The bacterial cell is resistant to the action of the enzymes and chemicals in the macrophage, and because the macrophage's outer surface hides the antigens on the surface of the bacterium, these intracellular bacteria can continue to reproduce without threat from the humoral

Figure 6.1 Tumor cells begin as normal host cells, but errors in the regulation of cell replication cause them to become cancer cells. These tumor cells have unique surface antigens as compared with normal cells, and the cell-mediated immune system recognizes them as "foreign." When a macrophage detects these tumor cells with their foreign antigens, they first bind the cells to their surface, then activate the processes to engulf and chemically destroy the tumor cell, as can be seen in this electron micrograph of a macrophage surrounding three tumor cells (SEM, X 3,000).

immune system. Macrophages actually contain both MHC-I and MHC-II complexes. Either one or both can be used to present foreign antigens. Thus, cytotoxic T cells will sometimes eliminate macrophages.

NON-B, NON-T CELLS

There is a third group of lymphocytes that are neither B cells nor T cells. Not surprisingly, these are called non-B, non-T lymphocytes. These cells are **natural killer (NK) cells**. Like

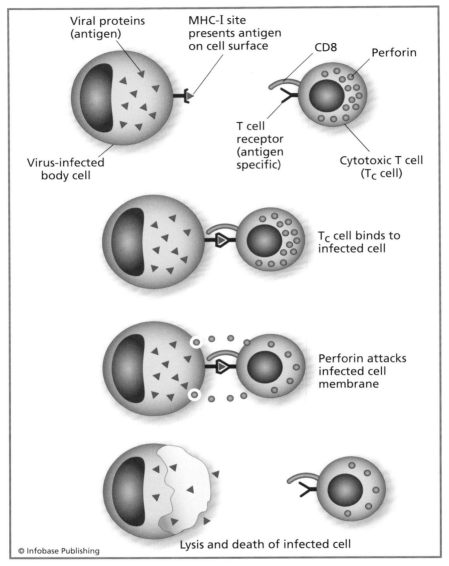

Viral proteins
(antigen)

MHC-I site
presents antigen
on cell surface

CD8

Perforin

T cell
receptor
(antigen
specific)

Virus-infected
body cell

Cytotoxic T cell
(T_C cell)

T_C cell binds to
infected cell

Perforin attacks
infected cell
membrane

Lysis and death of infected cell

© Infobase Publishing

Figure 6.2   If a host cell becomes infected with a virus, antigens from the virus are presented on the surface of the infected cell at MHC-I complexes. The presence of this antigen recruits cytotoxic T cells that are programmed to recognize the presented antigen. Cytotoxic T cells bind to the infected cell through the CD8 receptor on its surface and the MHC-1/antigen complex on the infected cell. Once the CD8 receptor binds, the cytotoxic T cell produces and secretes proteins called perforins. These proteins embed in the cell membrane of the infected host cells, creating holes in the membrane that ultimately cause the infected cell to rupture and die.

cytotoxic T cells, they lyse human cells by producing and secreting perforins. These cells kill virus-infected host cells and certain cancer cells. They are also very important in the rejection of transplanted tissues. The mechanism by which NK cells recognize foreign, infected, and cancer cells is unknown. The targeted cells must be presenting foreign antigens, but NK cells do not have receptors for specific antigens.

IMMUNE TOLERANCE

It would seem a risky proposition to have T cells that kill our own host cells. How are we sure that the immune system will not turn on us and attack our healthy cells? In some cases it does. These situations will be discussed in Chapter 8. Because the production of antibodies is a random assortment of cassettes in the antibody genes, why do we not make B cells and T cells that attack host tissue? Our immune system has an amazing ability to recognize its own, or "self," antigens. This is called *immune tolerance* because the immune system usually does not attack these tissues. The process is not fully understood, but we do know that as B cells and T cells are activated in the bone marrow and thymus, respectively, if self antigens are present, the B or T cells that would respond to that antigen are destroyed through a process called *apoptosis*, or programmed cell death. In a healthy individual there will be lots of self antigens around and very few foreign antigens. As a result, any lymphocyte that could attack a host tissue is destroyed before it can amplify.

CONNECTIONS

In this chapter, we have seen that infected cells and cancer cells present a danger to the host organism. If unchecked, they will destroy many other cells and may lead to death. Cytotoxic T cells react to specific foreign antigens on the surface of

(continues)

(continued)

infected host cells and produce perforins, which punch holes in that cell, resulting in its destruction. By doing so, the cell is eliminated before the virus or bacterium can reproduce or before the cancer cells can spread. By sacrificing a few cells the cell-mediated immune system protects the majority of others. We have also seen that there are some killer cells that do not look for a specific antigen but somehow know when a cell is infected or cancerous. The NK cells attack with perforins and destroy the dangerous cell before it can do more harm.

7

Importance of Vaccines

WHAT IS IMMUNITY?

Immunity IS A PHYSICAL STATE OF THE BODY THAT MAKES IT resistant to a particular disease. When you have immunity, you have B cells and antibodies and/or T cells that attack organisms that cause disease before they have a chance to establish infection. There are actually four different kinds of immunity depending on whether the immunity is a direct result of the activity of the immune system (active) or from "borrowed" antibodies (passive) and whether it is acquired by a natural process or an artificial one.

Passive artificial immunity occurs when a person is injected with antibodies from someone else. For instance, if someone in your family were to develop hepatitis, a liver disease caused by a virus, you and everyone else in your family might be advised to get *gamma globulin* shots. This involves receiving mixed serum from the blood of a number of different people. If one of those people has previously been exposed to hepatitis, they will have antibodies in their serum against the virus. When the antibody is injected into you, you will be protected by the antibodies as long as they last—usually a few weeks. Another example of

(continues on page 76)

THE DOCTOR, THE MILKMAID, AND THE BOY: A TRUE TALE

There are hundreds of human diseases, but none has been more devastating and feared than smallpox. However, you may have never heard of this disease. Although smallpox was quite prevalent and responsible for millions of deaths before the late twentieth century, the disease no longer exists.

During the seventeenth century, smallpox was epidemic in Europe. Major outbreaks in some cases killed one-third of the population of many towns and cities. However, inhabitants of Asia and Africa had been using an ancient method of preventing the disease. This practice, called variolation (from the formal name for the smallpox virus, *Variola major*), involved placing scab material from a survivor of smallpox into a tiny cut in the skin of a healthy person. Usually the healthy person developed a mild form of the disease but recovered. Those who recovered from the disease seemed to be resistant to future outbreaks of smallpox. This method was introduced to Europe by Lady Montague, the wife of the British ambassador to Turkey.

In 1796, a country physician named Edward Jenner noticed that milkmaids seemed to be particularly resistant to smallpox. He soon discovered that all of these disease-resistant women had contracted a mild skin disorder that resulted in the formation of one or a few scabs, usually on the hands. He also discovered that the cows were subject to a skin disease called cowpox and that it was this disease, caused by a virus related to, but not identical to, the smallpox virus that the dairy maids had contracted.

Jenner hypothesized that if a person had a case of cowpox, he or she became resistant to smallpox. One of his patients, a young milkmaid named Sarah Nelms, agreed to allow Jenner to scrape some of the scab material from a cowpox wound on her hand. Jenner then used this material to inoculate (infect) 8-year-old James Phipps, another patient from the village who had never been exposed to smallpox (Figure 7.1). Other than feeling a bit sick, James had no other ill effects except for a blister at the site of the inoculation. Later, Jenner subjected James to variolation with scab material from a patient with smallpox. The boy did not become ill. Jenner repeated the variolation

Figure 7.1   Edward Jenner, an English physician, is credited with discovering the first effective vaccine. By taking a small amount of the wound material from a cowpox pustule and introducing it into a healthy individual through a number of scratches on the skin, Jenner created a cowpox infection (Vaccinia) at the inoculation site. Once recovered from this mild, local infection, the person immunized was resistant to smallpox. The term *vaccine*, which we use for any artificial method to activate the immune system, is derived from the Latin word *vaccinus*, which means "of the cow." In this painting, Jenner is vaccinating his first patient, James Phipps.

process on James. There was no sign of smallpox, not even a mild case. The cowpox exposure had made James resistant to smallpox.

Jenner called the treatment "vaccination." *Vacca* is the Latin word for "cow." Very quickly, Edward Jenner's vaccination procedure became standard treatment to prevent smallpox. Because the cowpox virus and the smallpox virus are closely related, immunity to cowpox also provides protection against smallpox. The procedure remained the preferred way to protect from smallpox for more than 300 years. A few patients would have severe reactions to cowpox vaccination, and a very low number would die, but the risk was much lower of dying from vaccination than from a natural case of smallpox.

(continued from page 73)

passive artificial immunity is in the treatment of poisonous snake bites. If you are bitten by a rattlesnake or copperhead (or any of a number of other snakes that make venom), the doctor may give you an injection of antitoxin. This is usually serum from an animal, a goat for instance, that has been exposed to the snake toxin. The goat antibodies will bind to the venom, isolating it and preventing it from damaging your tissues. The problem with this process is that goat antibodies are foreign to your body. You can take this treatment once, but your immune system will probably then make antibodies against the goat antibodies. If you are ever given goat serum again, you run the risk of a serious, even life-threatening reaction.

Passive natural immunity is most commonly seen in infants. When a baby is first born, its immune system is not fully developed, and it cannot make its own antibodies. Fortunately, before the baby is born, antibodies from the serum of the mother enter its blood. Thus, the baby has its mother's immunity for the first few weeks. This window of borrowed protection from the mother is further extended if the baby is breast fed. The mother secretes IgA molecules in her breast milk, which enter the baby's body and protect her or him from disease.

Active natural immunity occurs when you are exposed to an infectious organism for the first time. You will probably get sick, but your body turns on the immune system for many diseases, providing protection against that same microbe in the future. The major childhood diseases (measles, mumps, German measles, and chickenpox) are all examples of diseases you typically get only once.

Active artificial immunity results from vaccination. There are now vaccines for many of the more common human diseases. A vaccine is introduced into the body of a healthy person, usually by injection. The immune system reacts to the foreign vaccine and makes antibodies against it. When those antigens are seen again in the future, the immune system immediately responds, blocking the organism from causing disease. Vaccinia virus, which causes cowpox, is used in a vaccine for smallpox. In this case, a live virus is introduced below the skin of a healthy person. The virus causes a mild disease, but the antibodies the body produces as a result of this process protect against the much more serious smallpox virus. This is called a "live vaccine," but there are other types of vaccines.

TYPES OF VACCINES

The live vaccine used to prevent smallpox is unusual because a virus that causes one disease is used to protect against another disease. However, there are not always related viruses that we can use to protect against human illness. An alternative type of vaccine is made from an attenuated, or weakened, microorganism. An attenuated microorganism is one that has been transferred through a series of individual animals that are not good hosts for that microbe. Over time, the virus becomes weakened so that its presence still causes an immune response, but it does not cause the disease. You can then use the attenuated virus in vaccinations. This has been done effectively for a number of diseases, including rabies. Unfortunately, sometimes attenuated organisms will mutate back to forms that cause serious disease. For that reason, attenuated vaccines must be carefully monitored.

Vaccines can also be made by chemically altering a microrganism so that it can no longer cause disease but can retain enough of its antigens to cause an immune response that immunizes you against future cases of the disease. Treating bacteria or viruses with formaldehyde is a common way to alter the organism so that it no longer reproduces, yet it retains enough of its original nature to turn on the immune system.

Finally, in the past few years scientists have developed vaccines from only parts of a microorganism. This is done by cloning the gene for an important surface protein for the bacterium or virus and injecting just that one protein into the patient.

SMALLPOX AND THE FUTURE

Around the middle of the twentieth century, scientists and physicians determined that because smallpox (Figure 7.2) could infect only humans, if a massive vaccination effort could be orchestrated globally, it might be possible to eradicate the virus that causes smallpox. The World Health Organization, the public health authority for the United Nations, took up the smallpox challenge, and by the mid-1970s, the last natural case of smallpox was recorded. The medical community had done something that had never before been accomplished. They had completely eliminated a human disease. This was accomplished through a massive vaccination program, focusing on all the people that lived in the area immediately around smallpox outbreaks. Because there was now a higher risk of dying from vaccination than from being exposed to smallpox, the vaccination program was terminated. You may know someone who received a smallpox vaccination. Usually the person will have a scar on the upper left arm, the site where cowpox was introduced into the body with several shallow point needles.

The elimination of smallpox was a modern miracle. The world scientific community discussed destroying all stocks of the smallpox virus, but decided that two stocks would be maintained should there ever be another smallpox outbreak. One stock was maintained in the United States, at the Centers for Disease Control and Prevention (CDC) in Atlanta, Georgia. The other was maintained in a laboratory in Russia. Since the fall of the Soviet Union, there are now concerns that the Russian smallpox stock may have been compromised and the virus could be in the hands of persons who would use it as a weapon or as a tool of terror. The risk of smallpox has returned, and the government of the United States is now determining how to reinstate a vaccination program. Those scars on the left arm may soon reappear as a testament to our failure to protect the world from this killer virus.

Figure 7.2   Smallpox was once one of the most feared diseases of humanity. About one in three people who contracted the disease died, and those that survived were permanently scarred from the pustules that formed from the infection. The young boy in this picture is suffering from smallpox. Although smallpox has been eliminated, stocks of the virus were maintained for research purposes. Some officials feel that if the stocks fall into the wrong hands, the disease could be used as a biological weapon.

If antibodies are made to the protein, those antibodies will protect you from the intact organism. We have also developed ways to use DNA and other components of the microbial cell to make vaccines.

HOW ARE VACCINES ADMINISTERED?

Vaccines have been traditionally administered through injection. In some cases, the vaccine is injected just below the skin (subcutaneously), and, in other cases, it is injected into muscle (intramuscularly). Both methods allow for the antigen or antigens in the vaccine to diffuse into the bloodstream slowly, allowing a continuous activation of the immune system over several days. In order to amplify the number of B and T cells that respond to the vaccine, multiple vaccinations may be required over weeks or months. In all cases where vaccines are injected, the majority of the antibody raised is in the bloodstream, usually in the form of IgG, although low levels of antibody can be found on the mucous membranes (usually IgA) and in other locations throughout the body (the specific immunoglobulin type at these other locations varies).

In recent years, the notion of localized immunization has gained popularity. Most microbes have specific sites where they enter the body. For example, pathogenic microbes that cause infections of the mouth, nose, throat, and lungs (respiratory pathogens) usually gain entry to the body by crossing the mucous membranes. New vaccines have been developed that are given as a nasal spray. These have proven as effective as injections in raising levels of antibody in the blood, but more importantly, inhaled vaccines raise a very active immune response at the mucous membranes themselves. This ensures that the antibodies bind the microbes just as they are entering the body, thus reducing the degree of damage that results to the tissues. There are also efforts to develop ingested vaccines to protect against diseases of the intestinal tract. Applying the vaccine through the same portal of entry as the microbes the vaccines are designed to fight speeds up the response time of the immune system and its efficiency.

CONNECTIONS

In this chapter, we have learned that there are a number of ways to acquire antibodies. They can be produced in the body naturally after exposure to antigens or through the use of vaccines. Antibodies can also be obtained from others, either as injected serum or, in the case of an infant, from the mother either before birth or through breast milk. Vaccines can be from live microbes, weakened microbes, inactivated microbes, or parts of microbes. Finally, although most vaccines are currently given by injection, new methods of delivering vaccines to the site where the microbe enters the body may be very effective in preventing disease.

8

Allergies and Autoimmune Diseases

ALLERGIC REACTIONS

Some of the most common problems that result from a functional immune system are allergies. Allergic reactions are uncomfortable and annoying but seldom cause serious harm. However, some rare allergic reactions can be life-threatening. Allergic reactions occur when the body comes in contact with an antigen that activates an immune response, resulting in a severe inflammatory response. Recall that when we discussed antibodies, or immunoglobulins, we mentioned that IgE antibodies are particularly involved in allergic reactions. IgE molecules look very much like IgG molecules except that they have a different constant region. The constant region of the IgE molecule binds receptor sites on mast cells and granulated white blood cells. In the absence of an antigen attached at the variable region of IgE, the immunoglobulin does not bind these cells, but when antigens are bound at the variable regions (the arms of the "Y"), the proteins making up the immunoglobulin shift, exposing the site that binds mast cells and granular leukocytes. When the antibody molecules bind to these cells, the cells release their granules, including histamine, a very powerful inflammatory mediator.

When histamine is released, it immediately initiates the inflammatory response. The capillaries become leaky, and fluid leaks into the tissues around the antigen/antibody complex, causing swelling, reddening, and heat. Additionally, the increased fluid stimulates nerve cells in the area, causing a severe itching sensation. In some cases, such as a skin rash, the inflammatory condition may not be life-threatening, but it can be uncomfortable. In other cases, it can cause damage to certain organs. In a few cases of allergic reaction, the inflammatory response can be so severe and so much fluid can leak from the circulatory system that the blood pressure drops and the body can enter a life-threatening condition. Most often these life-threatening reactions, called **anaphylactic reactions** (Figure 8.1), occur when the antigen is introduced into the blood or deeper tissues. This condition requires immediate intervention. Anaphylactic reactions can occur to foods, drugs, or even bee stings. If a person is severely allergic to certain foods, he or she must avoid them or run the risk of dying from the allergic reaction. In cases of bee stings, a person cannot always avoid exposure to bee venom. Most people with severe reactions to bees will carry a syringe filled with epinephrine. When injected, epinephrine causes an immediate block of the inflammatory response. In still other cases of allergies, a person may be able to minimize symptoms by taking antihistamines. These drugs block the action of histamine, thus preventing the inflammatory response. In some cases, cortisones are given; these drugs short-circuit the immune system, thus reducing inflammation and all its symptoms.

HAY FEVER

A very common form of allergic reaction is hay fever. If you have allergies to dust, dust mites, molds, or pollens, you can inhale them when they are in the air. Once in the respiratory tract, these allergens stimulate an inflammatory response, which leads to swelling of the tissues of the nose, throat, and

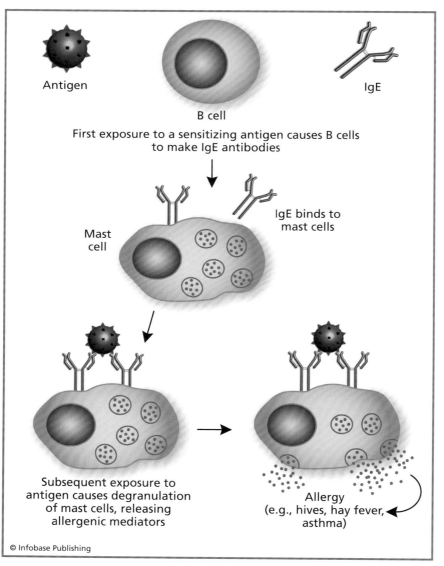

Antigen

B cell

IgE

First exposure to a sensitizing antigen causes B cells
to make IgE antibodies

IgE binds to
mast cells

Mast
cell

Subsequent exposure to
antigen causes degranulation
of mast cells, releasing
allergenic mediators

Allergy
(e.g., hives, hay fever,
asthma)

© Infobase Publishing

Figure 8.1   When a person allergic to a particular antigen is first
exposed, special B cells produce IgE antibodies. These antibodies are
structurally like IgG, but have a different constant region. The constant
region of the IgE molecule binds to receptors on mast cells. The next
time the foreign antigen is experienced by the host, the IgE molecules
bind to the variable regions (the "arms"). This stimulates the attached
mast cell to degranulate (release its stores of allergic mediators, such as
histamine). These mediators cause inflammatory responses.

CONFIDENCE AND CAMPING: A TRUE STORY

The following is a recollection by author Dr. Gregory J. Stewart: "As a teenager, I worked one summer at a Boy Scout camp in north Georgia. One of my duties was to teach the requirements for Second Class and First Class scouts. One of the topics required at that time was plant identification, particularly those plants that were poisonous and should be avoided when camping. While following one of the nature trails, I pointed out to my class the three-leafed poison ivy and poison oak plants. I explained that these plants contain an oil that causes allergic reactions in many people. One particularly arrogant scout announced to everyone that he was not allergic to poison ivy, and before I could stop him, he grabbed a handful of leaves, rubbed them all over his body, then put them in his mouth, chewed, and swallowed!

The next morning the young man was a sight to see. His face was so swollen that he could not open his eyes. A red rash covered his body, and because he had swallowed leaves, his throat was swollen to the point that he was having difficulty breathing. He had to be rushed to the local hospital, admitted, and intubated so he could breathe. He then began a series of painful injections of cortisones, compounds that short-circuit the immune system, in an effort to reduce the reaction.

This young man learned an important lesson. Just because you do not display an allergic reaction the first time you are exposed to an antigen does not mean you never will. The oil in poison ivy and poison oak plants is a huge molecule with hundreds of different antigens. A first, second, or even third exposure, if minor, might not have caused an allergic reaction, but each time you are exposed to one of these multi-antigenic molecules, you run the risk of activating an immune reaction. In this case, the immune reaction does not help the body; it harms it and, in some cases, can be fatal."

lungs. As the tissues swell with fluid, they close off the airway, making it hard to breathe and causing the symptoms of a "stuffy nose." The release of fluids may also cause your nose to run and your eyes to tear, and the inflammation in the area will often cause the nose and eyes to turn red. If you have a relatively mild case of hay fever, you can probably manage it with nose sprays and antihistamines. If the case is more serious, you may require an inhaler to reduce the swelling of the tissues around the airway, allowing you to breathe more easily. In some cases, the allergic reactions are so bad, your doctor may send you to an allergist for allergy shots.

What exactly are allergy shots and how do they work? One of the first things the allergist will do is to determine exactly which allergens are the problem. She or he will do this by placing small amounts of the most common allergens—plant pollens, molds, dust mites, and a variety of other agents— under the skin at a spot that has been labeled with the code for that particular antigen (Figure 8.2). A standard allergy screen will usually involve 50 or so different allergens, a negative control (usually water), and a positive control (histamine). These allergens are introduced with pins dipped in the allergen, and then pricked into the skin. The allergist will place most of these specimens on your back and some on your arms. If a particular spot turns red, swollen, and itchy within 24 to 48 hours, you are allergic to that allergen.

Once the allergist knows what allergens cause the problem, he or she will order a special mixture of these allergens at very low concentrations. Allergy shots are mixtures of the allergens to which you are allergic. The allergens are injected repeatedly and in increasing amounts. After a while, your body begins to think the allergen is a normal "self" protein. Suppressor T cells, the third class of T cells, target the cytotoxic T cells that bind that antigen and, more importantly, the B cells that produce antibodies against the allergen. Eventually, if all works well, the T and B cell lines that cause the allergic reaction are destroyed. Once this process is complete, the allergic reactions lessen, and the allergen is tolerated without an extreme response.

Figure 8.2   People suspected of having allergies often go to an allergist to determine the source of the allergy and the appropriate treatment. Allergy testing involves introducing a small amount of a suspected allergen under the skin. If the patient is allergic to the allergen, a localized inflammatory response occurs at the site of injection, causing the area to become red and swollen and to itch. Allergists will usually use a "panel" of two dozen or more of the most common allergens to test the patient. This will usually be administered by creating a grid on the back and arms with markers and testing a different allergen in each area. These allergens are introduced by pricking the skin with a small pin or needle that has a small amount of the allergen on its tip.

AUTOIMMUNE DISEASES

Recall that the body normally eliminates the T cells and B cells that can react with normal "self" proteins. This happens during fetal development and early childhood, and, as a result, the immune system does not attack body tissues. Unfortunately, in some cases the body fails to eliminate the B and T cells that recognize its own antigens. This leads to some very serious diseases collectively known as autoimmune diseases. In the following sections, we will look at some of the more common autoimmune diseases.

JUVENILE DIABETES

You may have friends who have diabetes and have had this ailment since they were small children. Chances are that these friends have juvenile diabetes, also called insulin-dependent or Type I diabetes. Most people with Type I diabetes develop it between the ages of four and six. We know there is a genetic basis for the disease because children of parents with juvenile diabetes have a much higher risk of the disease than children of parents who do not have the disease. Diabetes is a condition in which the body either stops producing insulin (Type I) or stops responding to insulin (Type II). Insulin is a hormone that controls the level of glucose in the blood. If glucose levels get too high, the pancreas secretes insulin into the bloodstream where it stimulates muscle cells to take up and burn glucose. This restores the glucose to normal levels. If your body does not get rid of excess glucose, you will become tired, you will not think clearly, and you may become grouchy. Because people with juvenile diabetes do not make insulin, they must take injections of insulin, often multiple times a day. They must carefully monitor what they eat and how much exercise they perform in order to balance the amount of insulin they give themselves. If they give themselves too little insulin, the glucose levels will get too high, and this can result in damage to the circulatory system, eyes, and kidneys. If they give themselves too much insulin, the glucose levels will drop to dangerously low levels, which can put them into shock. As you can see, diabetes is a serious disease that requires careful management, but what does it have to do with the immune system?

People with juvenile diabetes do not have a gene that will allow them to destroy B cells that make antibodies against the islet cells of the pancreas. As a result, the body makes antibodies and cytotoxic T cells that attack these cells, which are the cells that produce insulin. Juvenile diabetes is an autoimmune disease because the body's immune system destroys the cells that make insulin.

Rheumatoid Arthritis

Have you ever met anyone with rheumatoid arthritis? If so, the chances are you noticed that the joints, particularly those of the fingers and hands, are swollen and may be disfigured (Figure 8.3). Rheumatoid arthritis is another autoimmune disease. The skeletal system contains soft tissues on the ends of the bones that serve as cushions. This prevents the bones from grinding against one another when you move. In the case of rheumatoid arthritis, the body makes antibodies that attack these soft tissues, causing a massive inflammatory reaction at the site of the joints. The constant swelling resulting from the inflammation causes joint pain and the formation of swollen knots at the joints. Eventually, it causes damage to the bones themselves, resulting in disfigurement. Like most disabling autoimmune diseases, the only way to treat this condition is to block the actions of the immune system. This reduces the pain and damage from inflammation, but it makes the patient more susceptible to infection. As a result, patients under treatment for rheumatoid arthritis tend to get sick more often than people who do not have to suppress their immune systems. If left untreated, the inflammation at the joints may completely destroy the joints and bones, leading to permanent disability.

Lupus

The last example of an autoimmune disease we will discuss is lupus, often called systemic lupus because it affects the entire body. Lupus is an autoimmune disease in which antibodies and T cells target the connective tissue of the skin and internal organs, causing damage to the skin. Lupus is often characterized by unusual rashes with no apparent cause (Figure 8.4). As the antibodies attack the connective tissue, not only is the

Figure 8.3 Normally, the immune system distinguishes the body's own antigens as "self" and foreign antigens as "nonself." The system is programmed not to attack self antigens. In some cases, however, the immune system fails to recognize some self antigens and attacks body tissues. The resulting diseases, such as rheumatoid arthritis, are called autoimmune diseases. In this case, the immune system attacks the soft tissues that line and cushion the joints. The chronic inflammation causes the joints to swell and can result in deformation and accumulation of scar tissue. This image shows damage to the hand of an elderly patient who has suffered from rheumatoid arthritis for many years.

skin affected, but so too is the connective tissue of the inner organs. If untreated, this can lead to failure of one or more of the essential organs, resulting in death. Lupus is a progressive disease for which there is no cure. Management of lupus involves suppression of the immune system. As in the case of rheumatoid arthritis patients, lupus patients receiving immunosuppression therapy must be very careful to avoid infections because they are less able to fight off microbes.

Figure 8.4 Lupus is an autoimmune disease in which the immune system attacks the connective tissue of the skin. This figure illustrates a "butterfly rash" on the face of a lupus patient. This rash does not always occur in lupus cases, but it seldom occurs in non-lupus patients.

ARTIFICIAL AUTOIMMUNE RESPONSES

There are various antigens that may be found on the surface of the red blood cells. An artificial autoimmune response can be activated if the body is exposed to foreign antigens—ones not found on the red blood cells.

Blood Types
The ABO System

There are four main types of human blood. Types A and B each contain one type of antigen on the surface of the red blood cells. The third blood type, AB, has red blood cells with both A and B antigens. The fourth blood group, Type O, has neither A nor B antigens on the red cells.

People with Type A blood do not make antibodies against the A antigen because it is a "self" antigen; however, there is nothing to prevent them from making anti-B antibodies (antibodies that bind B antigens). Likewise, a person with Type B blood will have B antigens on the red blood cells and will not have anti-B antibodies in the serum, but could make anti-A antibodies. People with Type AB blood produce neither anti-A nor anti-B antibodies; therefore, they can receive any blood (A, B, AB, or O), and their bodies will not reject the blood. For this reason, persons with AB blood are called "universal recipients"—they can accept any of the major blood types. People with Type O can produce both anti-A and anti-B antibodies. As a result, they can safely receive only Type O blood; however, Type O blood can be donated to anyone because there are neither A nor B antigens on the cells to react with antibodies. This is why people with Type O blood are called "universal donors."

The Rh Factor

The antigens of the ABO system are not the only ones that must match for blood typing. Another important blood antigen is the Rh factor. People can either be Rh positive (Rh+) or Rh negative (Rh-). When blood is tested for a match, the Rh factor is checked as well as the ABO group. Consequently, a person can have a variety of blood types (A+, A-, B+, B-, AB+, AB-, O+, or O-, where the + or – represents the Rh factor). Rh factor can become a serious problem during pregnancy. If the mother of a fetus is Rh- and the father is Rh+, there is a 50% chance that the fetus will be Rh+ and a 50+ chance that it will be Rh-. If both the mother and the fetus are Rh- there are no problems, but if the mother is Rh- and the fetus is Rh+, the mother's immune system will recognize the blood of the fetus as foreign and will produce antibodies against it. This can lead to serious complications with the pregnancy, even resulting in the death of the baby. An injection can be given to the mother to prevent this problem. Both parents have their blood typed when there is a pregnancy so appropriate treatment can be given.

Blood Transfusions

If a patient is given a transfusion of the wrong type of blood, there may be very little reaction the first time (depending on how much blood they receive). The new blood cells have foreign antigens that will induce select B cells to secrete antibodies that will bind these cells. It may be that these blood cells are broken down before the antibodies can be produced. However, if the same patient is ever exposed to that foreign blood type again, the immune system will respond rapidly. Antibodies form clumps with the foreign blood cells (Figures 8.5a and 8.5b). This reduces the ability of the blood to transport oxygen, but perhaps more seriously, it can lead to blockage of the capillaries that supply blood and therefore oxygen to the vital organs. Damage to the vital organs can result, and death is not unusual. This is why doctors require that labs "type and cross match" any blood they give to a patient against a sample of the patient's own blood.

These tests will allow the lab technician or technologist to detect clumping if the bloods do not match, and a different unit of blood can be tested. In the case of emergencies in which there is no time to type and cross match blood, a doctor may give the patient saline (to raise the volume of fluid in the bloodstream), or units of O negative blood, which is least likely to cross react with serum in a patient's blood (the "negative" refers to the Rh factor).

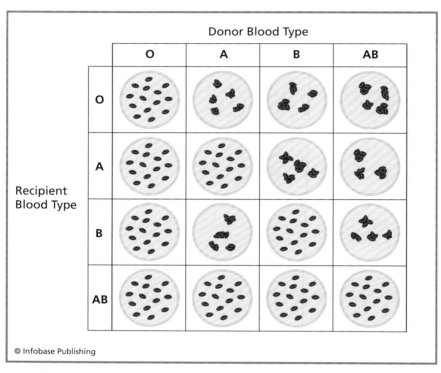

Figure 8.5a When a patient requires a blood transfusion, it is essential that the patient's blood and the donor's blood are typed and crossmatched. This test is done by taking a small amount of the patient's blood and mixing it with the available units of blood in the blood bank. Samples of each of the major blood groups are mixed with each other. Note that when blood of the same major blood groups are mixed (O with O, A with A, etc.), the red blood cells stay evenly distributed. Others, when mixed, form clumps of antibody and red blood cells, as can be seen when donor Type A is mixed with recipient Type B.

Unfortunately, not enough people donate blood. Sometimes the supply of blood becomes so low that surgeons have to cancel elective surgeries, and emergency patients have been known to die because not enough of the right blood type was available. For this reason, scientists are looking at new ways to meet the blood demand. Some are trying to develop artificial blood; this would not contain blood cells, but would

Figure 8.5b These samples will be tested to determine their blood group. During transfusions the blood group of the donated blood must be compatible with the patient's blood group. A positive reaction occurs when antibodies in the reagent attach to antigens on the surface of the red blood cells. This causes the red blood cells to clump as the antibodies bridge between cells, making many cells stick together. If this happens in the body, it can block small blood vessels, which can be fatal.

have other chemicals that could transport oxygen and carbon dioxide. Artificial blood could save many lives, but we have not succeeded in this effort so far. A more promising approach is blood type conversion. We now know there are enzymes that can remove the A and B antigens from red blood cells. Treating blood with these enzymes would result in essentially all blood being Type O. If we can find a way to remove all of the antigens from the surface of red blood cells without destroying the function of the cells, we can make blood typing obsolete. We would still need blood donors, but at least all units of blood could be given to all patients. Research continues in this area.

ORGAN TRANSPLANT REJECTION

The last example of a case where the immune system may harm more than help is in the area of organ transplants. Recall

ORGAN TRANSPLANTS

The immune system plays a critical role in organ transplants. The MHC antigens on the donor's organs must match those present in the recipient or the recipient's body will attack the new organs. Even with a nearly perfect match, there is still a chance of rejection.

Recently, the delicacy of organ transplantation made national headlines when a young girl received a mismatched heart-lung transplant. She had spent three years on the donor waiting list as a result of a heart deformity that prevented her lungs from depositing oxygen in her blood.

However, what seemed like a routine transplant needed to save this girl's life became a complicated test of scientific know-how. When the Donor Services contacted the doctor in charge, they had another potential recipient in mind for the available organs. Because the first patient was not ready for transplant, the doctor inquired as to whether the heart and lungs might be available for the young girl. Unfortunately, Donor Services and the doctor never discussed blood-type compatibility. Donor and recipient matching is divided into three main areas: blood type matching, tissue matching, and cross matching. Each qualification refers to both the donor and the recipient's condition. These tests used to determine a match are used to rate the overall expected success for the transplant.

In this young girl's case, the qualifications were overlooked, setting up an even more complicated situation for the young girl. Unfortunately, due to human error, organs that had Type A blood, which did not match her Type O+ blood, replaced her heart and lungs. Because of the mismatch, her body initially rejected the transplant. Soon after the surgery, the surgical team received a call that all cells in the body have the same MHC-I complexes on their surfaces. Different people can have different MHC complexes. Because all of the cells, and therefore all of the organs, are tagged with these MHC complexes, doctors have to match the donor and recipient MHC antigens as best they can before a patient can receive an organ transplant. If you receive an

from the hospital's Transplant Immunology Laboratory reporting the organs were incompatible with the girl's blood type. Doctors began plasmapheresis (separation of blood plasma components to remove immune-active components) and a high dose of immuno-suppressants, drugs that shut down the immune system in order to prevent organ rejection. The hospital immediately contacted the United Network for Organ Sharing about the ABO incompatibility and the girl's need for new organs.

Because of the severity of her situation, the young girl's name went to the top of the recipient list. Within two weeks of her first operation, which was unusually fast despite her priority status, a second set of organs was located. Soon thereafter the girl underwent her second heart-lung transplant. Doctors claimed that the organs were working perfectly after the second surgery and were hopeful about her chances. However, too much damage had been done to her body for her to recover. She had been near death by the time she underwent her second surgery. The treatment she received to prevent her body from rejecting the organs was necessary, but the length of time had greatly weakened her body. Following the second transplant, she experienced bleeding and swelling in her brain. Further tests revealed that there was no electrical brain activity and no blood flow to the brain. Shortly thereafter, the girl was removed from life support. Although the hospital has since changed its policies regarding transplant surgeries (now three members of the transplant team are required to confirm the compatibility of the donated organs with the organ recipient), controversy is still swirling around the tragedy of this girl's death. Hopefully, one tragedy can prevent the same accident from occurring again.

organ from someone with a different MHC complex, your body will recognize the organ as foreign and will attack it. This is what happens when a transplant patient "rejects" an organ. As much of a problem as blood donations can be, organ donations are an even bigger problem. Not nearly enough people donate their organs when they die. As a result, there are always many more people who need an organ than there are matching organs. Thousands of people die in this country every year because they cannot get matching organs when they need them. Because MHC complexes are genetically coded, persons of one race are more likely to have the same blood type and organ type as others in their race than people of different races.

Finding matching organs is particularly difficult for His-panic or African-American patients because people in these groups have traditions that make organ donation less likely. It is important to remember that in most cases (with the possible exception of kidney transplants and cornea transplants) organs are harvested from people who have recently died.

CONNECTIONS

As you have learned in this chapter, although the immune system is very important in avoiding and fighting infection, it can also be the source of health problems. There can be allergic reactions to pollen in the air, resulting in hay fever, or to certain foods or beverages that can cause problems ranging from a mild rash, to vomiting and nausea, to more life-threatening reactions. Some people are allergic to the proteins in things such as bee venom, where even a single bee sting may cause us to experience a life-threatening condition called anaphylaxis.

The immune system is also the source of most problems with blood transfusions and organ transplants. If the blood and organs are not carefully matched to the blood or tissues of the person receiving the transfusion or transplantation, the results can be deadly. Finally, in some cases, the immune system fails to recognize our own tissues and may produce antibodies that attack part of our own body. This can lead to long-term debilitating illnesses or in some cases, death.

The immune system is extremely powerful. It must be in order to fight infection, but when the normal checks and balances of the immune system are ignored or overridden by the body, the immune system may become our worst enemy rather than our close ally.

9

Immune Reactions as a Scientific Tool

DIAGNOSTIC IMMUNOLOGY

OUR UNDERSTANDING OF IMMUNOLOGY HAS CHANGED dramatically over the past 30 years. What was poorly understood in the 1980s has become one of the fastest growing and most significant areas of science. It has also become one of the most practical areas. Immunological processes are among the most common and most important diagnostic tests performed in the laboratory. Remember that antibodies (immunoglobulins) are extremely specific. A given antibody will bind only to a single antigen, or perhaps to a group of very closely related antigens. This high degree of specificity makes antibodies a powerful tool for detecting specific proteins, polysaccharides, and other large molecules. This specificity has allowed us to develop antibody-based reagents (supplies used in the laboratory) to detect specific molecules. We will explore some of the more common applications of antibodies for diagnostic tests.

PRECIPITATION REACTIONS

One of the first tests to be developed was the precipitation test. The basis of this test is simple. Every antibody molecule has two or more antigen-binding sites. These sites bind identical antigens. Cells, whether they are blood cells or bacterial cells, tend to have many copies of the same antigens on their cell surfaces. If you mix a suspension of these cells with serum containing an antibody for one of the surface antigens on the cells, the antibodies will begin binding to different cells, and because the cells have lots of antigen sites, they will bind multiple copies of antibodies. The cells very quickly clump together, forming large complexes that fall out of solution, or precipitate (Figure 9.1).

A practical example of the precipitation test is blood grouping. If you take a sample of Type B blood and mix a drop of that blood with serum containing anti-B antibodies, the blood cells will clump together. This will cause the normally even suspension of blood cells to become very "grainy" in appearance. The formation of grains of cells indicates that the blood cells contain the B antigen. If you mixed a drop of the same blood sample with serum containing anti-A antibodies, these antibodies would not bind the antigens on the blood cells, and the blood cells would remain evenly spread throughout the suspension. Blood from a person with Type AB blood would precipitate in both samples of serum, and Type O blood, which has neither A nor B antigens on its red blood cells, would not clump in either serum. With just two serum samples, one that binds the A antigen and one that binds the B antigen, we can distinguish the four major blood groups.

Another common precipitation test is the double diffusion test. This test involves small wells punched into a gel matrix. If you put serum against a particular antigen in the center well and you put protein (antigen) samples in several surrounding wells you can determine how related those protein samples are to one another. The antibodies in the serum diffuse into the gel, moving outward. The proteins in the surrounding wells diffuse through the gel toward the center well. When the antibody and an antigen that binds to it diffuse to the same place,

© Infobase Publishing

Figure 9.1   In this figure, IgM antibodies are added to antigens that bind at the variable regions. Note that all ten variable regions of the IgM antibody (two regions per "Y") bind the same antigen. The IgM antibody in this case binds a surface antigen on a bacterial cell. There are usually many copies of this antigen per cell. As a result, large complexes of antibody and antigen are formed. These large complexes of bacterial cells and antibodies are easily recognized by the immune system, allowing the body to eliminate invading bacteria quickly.

the proteins precipitate, creating a visible, milky band between the wells. These bands of precipitation appear only if the antigen in a well is bound by the antibody in the serum. If these two proteins do not bind together, they continue to diffuse and do not precipitate.

Scientists have been able to further improve precipitation tests by attaching microscopic latex beads to the constant end of the antibody. Because only the variable ends of the antibody bind antigen, adding a bead to the constant end does not interfere with the binding of the antigen and the antibody. Suppose that you have made an antibody that binds an antigen on the surface of the measles virus. Viruses are so small that you probably would not see the precipitation between virus particles and their antibodies; however, if you mix a patient sample that contains the measles virus with anti-measles antibodies with attached latex beads, the viruses will bind multiple antibodies, and the antibodies will bind multiple viruses. This causes the antibodies to concentrate together, and because the latex beads are attached to the antibodies, these will also be drawn together. As a result, if the antigen that reacts with the antibody is present in the patient sample (in this case, the antigens on the surface of the measles virus), the beads will form visible clumps. A similar method is used in the modern version of the Lancefield *Streptococcus* identification test (see box on page 110). Antibodies against the major Lancefield group polysaccharides are modified with latex beads. If the bacterial sample being tested is a Group B species, there would be a grainy spot in the area containing the anti-B serum, but not in any of the others.

FLUORESCENT ANTIBODIES

Certain chemicals have the ability to absorb energy from ultraviolet (UV) light. The energy of this light causes atoms in the chemicals to become excited (attain a higher energy level). When they return to their resting level, they release the excess energy but at a longer wavelength than that of the UV light used to excite the chemicals. When the wavelength of the released energy is in the visible range, you can actually see the chemicals glow under UV light (Figure 9.2). You may have seen this phenomenon demonstrated in a geology museum where certain minerals absorb UV light and give off visible light. The color of the visible light released depends on the chemical being excited. Specific chemicals often glow a particular color because they always release light of the same wavelength.

There are a number of chemicals commonly used to make antibodies fluorescent. Some glow red, others glow green, and still others glow different colors. These chemicals can be bound to the constant region of an antibody without interfering with the ability of the chemical to fluoresce. When used with a UV microscope, fluorescent antibodies become powerful tools for diagnosis.

For example, let's say you want to develop a test for cholera. Cholera is a serious disease that results in severe diarrhea. If left untreated, a person with cholera can die within days from dehydration. The first step in creating a fluorescent antibody test for cholera would be to make a suspension of killed cholera cells. These cells could not reproduce or cause disease, but would retain their surface antigens. If you injected the killed cells into a laboratory animal, you would soon find antibodies against cholera in the serum of the animal. If you isolated this antibody and attached a fluorescent molecule that glows red under UV light to the constant region of the anticholera antibody, you could detect the cholera bacterium because it would glow red under a UV microscope in the presence of the fluorescent antibody.

Why does the bacterium glow? The variable end of the antibody would bind to the surface antigens on the bacterium. Because there are many of these surface antigens, you would basically surround the cell with antibodies containing the fluorescent tags. As a result, there would be enough fluorescent chemical molecules around the cells to make the cell glow red. If, however, the patient had diarrhea from a different bacterium, the antibodies would not attach to the cells so the cells would not glow under the microscope. The specific nature of antigen-antibody reactions makes fluorescent antibodies very powerful tools for identification of specific

Figure 9.2   Fluorescent antibodies are powerful tools in modern medical diagnostics. Antibodies against a particular antigen (for instance, a particular protein) are chemically modified by adding a fluorescent dye to the constant end of the molecule. When the antibodies bind to the target, they concentrate around it in high numbers so that many fluorescent dye molecules surround the target. Under UV light the fluorescent dye molecules glow, and since the dye molecules surround the target, the target will appear to glow under the microscope, as seen here.

microorganisms. There are fluorescent antibody kits available for many of the most common disease-causing bacteria, fungi, and viruses.

ENZYME-LINKED ANTIBODY KITS

Another very powerful tool using antibodies is the enzyme-linked antibody. This is very similar to the fluorescent antibody test except that an enzyme is attached to the constant region of the antibody instead of a fluorescent chemical. Remember that an enzyme is a protein that drives a particular reaction. It is a biological catalyst. One commonly used enzyme for this purpose is horseradish peroxidase. A peroxidase is an enzyme that breaks down peroxide to oxygen and water. There are also certain chemicals that have peroxide groups on them that go from a colorless compound to a colored compound when peroxidase acts upon them. By isolating peroxidase from horseradish you can chemically attach the enzyme to the constant region of an antibody. When you do, any time an antibody binds to an antigen, it will carry the enzyme with it.

A good example of an enzyme-linked antibody test is the typical home pregnancy test. When a woman becomes pregnant, she produces certain protein hormones that are normally either absent or present in very low concentrations. These hormones can be detected in the urine of a pregnant woman. If a woman thinks she might be pregnant, she can take a urine sample and dip the end of a test dipstick into the urine sample. If she is pregnant, the concentration of the hormone will be relatively high and the hormone will stick to the dipstick. The antibody will then be added and will bind to the surface of the antigen on the dipstick. The substrate for peroxidase is also present in the mixture. If enough enzymes adhere to the dipstick because there is enough hormone present to bind the antibody, the concentration of peroxidase will be high enough to convert the enzyme substrate to a colored product. If the indicator on the test strip changes color, the chances of pregnancy are very high. As with fluorescent antibody kits, hundreds of commercial, enzyme-linked antibody tests are available for both home and laboratory use.

MONOCLONAL ANTIBODIES

We have seen a few examples of how antibodies can be used for specific diagnostic tests. Perhaps you are wondering how we get these antibodies. The most common method for making specific antibodies is the monoclonal procedure. Monoclonal means "one clone." In other words, monoclonal antibodies all come from clones of one antibody-producing cell.

If you inject a laboratory animal with a killed bacterial preparation, the animal's immune system will make antibodies against a large number of antigens on the surface of the bacterial cells. In addition, because that animal has been exposed to countless other foreign antigens, its serum will contain many antibodies with specificity for different antigens. This serum is called a polyclonal serum because it has antibodies to lots of different antigens. It would seem impossible for you to get a serum with only one specific antibody, and this is always the case when you use blood serum from an animal. So how do you get monoclonal antibodies? To do so, you have to isolate specific B cells and find a way to keep them growing in artificial media as a cell culture. The problem is that B cells can divide only a few times before the cells die. This is true for all cells, except for cancer cells. Cancer cells are said to be immortal. They keep reproducing as long as they have nutrients. The secret to making monoclonal antibodies is to fuse together a B cell with a cancer cell. The resulting cell is called a **hybridoma** (*hybrid* meaning "made of two different elements"; *oma* meaning "cancer cell.")

To begin this process, you start with a laboratory animal, most commonly a mouse. The mouse is injected with the antigen you want to detect. Let us assume we will use protein X as our antigen. We take a pure preparation of protein X and inject it under the skin of the mouse. Two weeks later we repeat this process and continue to do so every two weeks for about two months. At the end of that time, we take a small sample of blood from the mouse and test it to see if it has antibodies against protein X. Because we find that it does contain these antibodies, we know that the mouse is making B cells that produce antibodies that react with protein X.

After several injections of protein X, there are probably many B cells making that particular antibody because of the multiple rounds of B cell amplification. The next step is to isolate one or more of those B cells from all the others. You may remember that the spleen is one of the organs of the immune system. If we surgically remove the spleen from the mouse and break it down into individual cells, some of those will be B cells, and hopefully some of the B cells will be those programmed to make anti-protein X antibodies. We next separate the B cells from all other cells in the spleen tissue. Using a few chemical tricks, we can actually fuse the B cells to cancer cells called myeloma cells. These cells can reproduce continually. The resulting cells are hybridomas, fusions of cancer cells and B cells. These hybridoma cells have the properties of continual reproduction but contain the programmed gene for making the anti-protein X antibody.

Next, dilute the myeloma cells so that a small volume can be added to each of several small wells on a special tissue culture plate. Add tissue culture media to the wells and the hybridomas grow. As they do, they secrete antibodies. Some of these will be fusions from B cells that make anti-protein X antibody, but most will make other antibodies. How can we tell them apart? Allow the cells to grow for several hours. Soon the medium in the wells of the tissue culture plates will be filled with the antibodies made by that particular hydridoma.

In another tissue culture plate, add a small amount of protein X and cause it to attach to the bottom of the well in the plate. Next, take a small amount of serum from each of the wells of hybridomas and add each serum sample to a different well on the tissue culture plate. If the serum contains antibodies against something other than protein X, the antibodies will not bind to the protein, but if the antibodies have variable regions that bind protein X, the antibodies will stick to the protein and therefore stick to the well. Wash the wells out, and only the antibodies that specifically bind to protein X will stay in the well. All other antibodies wash away.

The next step is to determine which wells have antibodies in them. All the antibodies that we are testing are mouse IgG antibodies. Remember that this is a protein and the constant region of all mouse IgG antibodies are the same—that is, they have the same antigens in them. If we purify IgG from mouse serum and inject it into another animal—a goat, for example—the goat's immune system sees the mouse IgG as a foreign protein, and it makes antibodies that bind the constant region of the mouse antibody. If we then purify antibody from the goat and attach horseradish peroxidase to the constant region of the goat antibody, the variable region of the goat antibody will bind to the constant region of the mouse antibody. We take a sample of goat antibody with peroxidase attached and add it to each well in the second tissue culture plate, the one with protein X and the various fluid samples from our hybridomas. If there is mouse antibody in the well (this can only happen if the mouse antibody has bound to protein X), the goat antibody will bind the constant region of the mouse IgG molecule. Those wells with mouse IgG will bind the goat antibody, and those without it will not.

Once again we wash out the wells to remove any goat antibody that is not tightly fixed to the well through the mouse antibody and the protein X. This is called a "sandwich antibody technique" because it has different layers. Finally, we add a small amount of the peroxidase reagent to the wells. The wells with peroxide will change color only if the goat antibody is attached to the plate, which happens only if the mouse antibody is attached to protein X. This last event can occur only if the hybridoma in the well of the first tissue culture plate resulted from fusion of a B cell that makes an anti-protein X antibody. Because we know which well each serum sample came from, we can determine which hybridomas make the monoclonal antibodies we want. We can transfer these cells to larger tissue culture containers and make large amounts of antibody. We can also store some of the hybridoma cells in a very cold freezer and preserve them. In the future, when we need more antibody, we remove a frozen sample of the hybridoma, let it thaw, and transfer it to fresh tissue culture medium. The

REBECCA CRAIGHILL LANCEFIELD: A WOMAN AHEAD OF HER TIME

The sciences, until the past 40 years or so, were dominated by men. Microbiology and its related sciences are a notable exception to that rule. Women have played pivotal roles in the development of microbiology. One example of an early female pioneer of microbiology and immunology is Rebecca Craighill Lancefield (Figure 9.3). Dr. Lancefield developed an interest in a genus of bacteria, *Streptococcus*, very early in her career and continued to study this group for many years. The species of bacteria in this group were frequently associated with serious diseases, including strep throat, scarlet fever, and rheumatic fever. She found that the species of this group that could cause the most serious diseases were often **hemolytic**. That means if you grew them on agar plates (a solid medium for cultivation of bacteria) that contained whole red blood cells, these bacteria would cause the blood cells to lyse, creating a clear area around the growth area for the bacterium (blood agar is normally a cloudy red agar). Unfortunately, it was very difficult to tell one hemolytic species from another.

Dr. Lancefield soon discovered that different species of *Streptococcus* had different polysaccharides on their surfaces. Polysaccharides are large complex molecules made up of simple sugars connected together. These polysaccharides were big enough to be immunogenic. Dr. Lancefield began to purify the polysaccharides from each of the species she was studying and to use them to make antibodies. In 1933, she published a report in a scientific journal that proposed and demonstrated an immunological test to distinguish between different groups of *Streptococci* (plural for *Streptococcus*). She demonstrated that antibodies made against a specific polysaccharide from a species of this group could precipitate the antigens isolated from the bacteria. This could be observed visually on a microscope slide. Dr. Lancefield developed one of the most powerful tools for diagnosis of disease for her time. The contribution that Dr. Lancefield made lives on. Her Lancefield groups of *Streptoccoci* and her antibodies for their detection are still the definitive test for classifying pathogenic bacteria of this genus. Dr. Lancefield continued an impressive career. She became the second woman to serve as President of the Society of

Figure 9.3 Rebecca Lancefield was one of the most influential women in the history of microbiology. Her work with the serological types (different antigen types) of the genus *Streptococcus* in the 1930s developed a powerful tool for diagnosing many serious infections, including streptococcal pneumonia, strep throat, and Group B strep infections that are leading causes of deaths in newborns. The Lancefield typing system is still used today to classify species in this important genus of pathogens.

American Bacteriology, which later became the American Society for Microbiology, the oldest and largest biological society in the world. In 1961, she became the only woman to serve as President of the American Association of Immunologists, and in 1970, Dr. Lancefield was awarded one of the highest honors for science in the United

(continues on page 112)

(continued from page 111)

States when she was elected to the membership of the National Academy of Sciences and became only the twelfth female member of the Academy.

Dr. Lancefield left her mark on science. She was one of the first scientists to show a practical, diagnostic application for immunology. Her role as an immunologist and a scientist continues to inspire young women and men to enter the microbiological and immunological sciences.

hybridoma cells will grow and secrete more of our anti-protein B antibody. With a little care, we now have an unlimited supply of this specific antibody, and we can produce enough to make enzyme-linked tests or fluorescent antibody tests.

CONNECTIONS

As you have moved through this book you have learned which parts of the body make up the immune system, how the immune system works to help you and sometimes hurt you, and how we can use the power of the immune system to make very specific diagnostic tests. Perhaps some readers will consider a career in immunology. Immunology is one of the fastest growing and largest market areas in the biological sciences. Even with all we now know about the immune system, there is still much more to be learned. Perhaps you will be one of the future scientists who answer some of the remaining mysteries of our body's most fascinating system—the immune system.

Appendix: Conversion Chart

Unit (metric)		Metric to English		English to Metric	
LENGTH					
Kilometer	km	1 km	0.62 mile (mi)	1 mile (mi)	1.609 km
Meter	m	1 m	3.28 feet (ft)	1 foot (ft)	0.305 m
Centimeter	cm	1 cm	0.394 inches (in)	1 inch (in)	2.54 cm
Millimeter	mm	1 mm	0.039 inches (in)	1 inch (in)	25.4 mm
Micrometer	μm	1 - millionth of a meter			
WEIGHT (MASS)					
Kilogram	kg	1 kg	2.2 pounds (lbs)	1 pound (lbs)	0.454 kg
Gram	g	1 g	0.035 ounces (oz)	1 ounce (oz)	28.35 g
Milligram	mg	1 mg	0.000035 ounces (oz)		
Microgram	μg	1 - millionth of a gram			
VOLUME					
Liter	L	1 L	1.06 quarts	1 gallon (gal)	3.785 L
				1 quart (qt)	0.94 L
				1 pint (pt)	0.47 L
Milliliter	mL or cc	1 mL	0.034 fluid ounce (fl oz)	1 fluid ounce (fl oz)	29.57 mL
Microliter	μL	1 - millionth of a liter			
TEMPERATURE					
		$[°F] = [°C] \times 9/5 + 32$		$[°C] = ([°F] - 32) \times 5/9$	

Glossary

Acquired immune deficiency syndrome (AIDS)   A deadly disease that develops after infection with the human immunodeficiency virus (HIV).

Acquired immunity   A natural defense mechanism that seems limited to vertebrates; it involves the ability to identify molecules as foreign to the body and to produce specific proteins or cells for the removal of those foreign molecules.

Active artificial immunity   The development of antibodies or immune-active cells after deliberate exposure to a foreign material; development of immunity in response to a vaccine is an example of active artificial immunity.

Active natural immunity   The development of antibodies or immune-active cells as a result of a natural exposure to a foreign material; an example is development of immunity to a disease after having that disease.

Alternate complement pathway   A series of proteins found in the serum of the blood. These proteins initiate a cascade of reactions that are independent of antibodies. Ultimately, the proteins create holes in infecting bacterial or other foreign cells that lead to cell lysis.

Anaphylactic reaction   An immune reaction, usually to a foreign antigen found in the blood, that sets off a severe inflammatory response; blood pressure drops rapidly and death can result.

Antibody   A protein made by B lymphocytes that has the ability to bind to specific foreign antigens; the attachment of antibodies to a foreign material leads to its destruction by the body.

Antigen   A molecule that has a particular surface structure that is bound by an antibody.

B cells   White blood cells in the lymphoid family that are central to the humoral immune system; they develop into plasma cells, which produce antibodies, and memory cells, which retain the ability to make antibodies if a particular antigen is experienced in the future.

B cell amplification   A series of events controlled by lymphokines; a B cell with the ability to bind a particular antigen is stimulated to reproduce when the antigen is presented to it. During reproduction, these B cells differentiate into plasma cells and memory cells.

Basophil   A white blood cell in the polymorphonucleocyte family. These cells contain granules that contain histamine, heparin, and a number of other chemicals that stimulate an inflammatory response; the granules bind basic dyes.

Cell-mediated immunity   A form of acquired immunity in which cytotoxic T cells recognize body cells that have become compromised either by becoming cancerous or by viral infection; the cytotoxic T cells release perforins that create holes in the compromised host cells and result in cell lysis and cell death.

Classical complement pathway   A series of sequential reactions of proteins found in blood serum; these proteins initiate the reaction sequence by binding to foreign cells with attached antibodies, eventually leading to the lysis of the foreign cells.

Complement proteins   The group of blood serum proteins that are involved in the complement cascade reactions.

Complement system   See **Complement proteins**.

Cytotoxic T Cell   Antigen-specific T cells that bind to body cells that are infected with viruses or have become cancerous; cytotoxic C cells release perforins that lead to lysis of the compromised cells.

Eosinophil   Specific white blood cells of the polymorphonucleocyte family that contain granules that bind acidic dyes; the granules contain powerful enzymes and chemicals that can destroy invading foreign cells, including those of fungi, protozoa, and worms.

Epithelial cells   The class of human cells that make up the layers of the skin and mucous membranes.

Erythrocytes   Red blood cells.

Hematopoiesis   The production of blood cells.

Hemolytic   Having the ability to lyse red blood cells; usually due to the presence of enzymes called hemolysins or lipases.

Human immunodeficiency virus (HIV)   An RNA virus commonly believed to be the cause of AIDS.

Humoral immune system   The specific cells and cell products that lead to the production of antibodies; B cells, T-helper cells, and macrophages are all important in the humoral immune system.

Hybridoma   A cell made by fusing one cell type to a carcinoma (cancer) cell; used in the production of monoclonal antibodies by fusing B cells to carcinoma cells. Hybridomas can be grown indefinitely in tissue culture.

Immunity   The ability to resist infection.

Immunogen   Antigens that are large enough to trigger antibody production against one or more sites on the immunogen; all immunogens are antigens, but some antigens are too small to be immunogens.

Immunoglobulin (Ig)   The class of blood proteins produced by B cells that is commonly referred to as antibodies; there are five distinct classes of human immunoglobulins.

Inflammation   See **Inflammatory response**.

Inflammatory mediators   Chemicals that stimulate the immune response; some inflammatory mediators are made by the body, others are components of foreign cells, such as bacteria.

Inflammatory response   A series of nonspecific reactions that result from damage to tissues or infection by foreign micro-organisms. Blood vessels dilate causing fluid to leak from the circulatory system into the tissues surrounding the damaged/infected area, resulting in swelling, reddening, warmth, and pain at the site.

Innate immune system   A series of inborn defense mechanisms to infection that do not require previous exposure to a particular antigen.

Interleukins   Proteins produced by one type of white blood cell that serve as signal molecules to communicate or stimulate other white blood cells.

Leukocytes   White blood cells.

Lymph   Fluid derived from blood plasma that bathes the tissues outside the circulatory system. It transports immune-active proteins and cells in the tissues and eventually flows back into the circulatory system through the lymphatic vessel network.

Lymphatic system   System that includes cells (lymphocytes), lymph vessels, lymph nodes, and tissues and organs, including the tonsils, adenoids, thymus, and spleen.

Lymphatic tissue   Clusters of tissue that play important roles in immune response. These tissues are less differentiated than organs, but they exist as a complex of cells unlike B and T cells. Tonsils, adenoids, and Peyer's patches are all examples of lymphatic tissue.

Lymphoid family   The group of white blood cells that contains the B cells and T cells or those cells directly involved in the acquired immune response.

Lysozyme   An enzyme produced in human tears that breaks down the structural molecule of bacterial cell walls.

Major histocompatibility complex (MHC)   Proteins found on the surface of all cells; they are important in self-recognition"and play a critical role in normal immune function and in organ transplant rejection. MHC-I functions in antigen presentation during cell-mediated immune response; MHC-II is present almost exclusively on phagocytic cells and is essential in presentation of foreign antigens to activate the humoral (antibody-based) immune system.

MALT   See **Mucosa-associated lymphoid tissue**.

Macrophages   Large white blood cells that develop when neutrophils leave the circulatory system and enter the surrounding tissues. These are phagocytic cells that ingest and break down microorganisms and other foreign antigens.

Mast cells   A type of immune cell that releases histamine when stimulated by an allergen.

Memory cell   A lymphoid cell derived from a B cell upon first activation; these cells are remain in the body and are stimulated to replicate and to make new plasma cells upon subsequent exposure to a specific foreign antigen.

Microorganism   Generally a single-celled living organism too small to see without magnification. Major groups include bacteria, fungi, protozoa, algae, and viruses.

Monocyte   The most common form of agranular white blood cell; they contain one nucleus.

Mononuclear leukocyte   See **Monocyte**.

Mucosa-associated lymphoid tissue (MALT)   Patches of lymphoid tissue found just below the mucous membranes

Mucus   A thick, sticky polymer that coats the mucous membranes, entrapping foreign material such as dust, bacteria, and fungi, therefore preventing them from penetrating into deeper tissues.

Mucous membranes   The membranes that line the respiratory, digestive, and reproductive tracts, as well as the sockets of the eyes.

Natural killer (NK) cells   Non-B, non-T cells that lyse certain human cells by the production of perforins.

Neutrophil   The predominant form of white blood cells; they stain poorly and contain powerful enzymes that destroy foreign materials.

Nonspecific reactive responses   Immune responses that do not require a specific antigen for initiation.

Null lymphocytes   Lymphocytes that have not differentiated into B or T cells.

Passive artificial immunity   A form of borrowed immunity in which a person obtains antibodies made by another person; the most common example is receipt of immunoglobulin injections to ward off infection.

Passive barrier defenses   Physical structures, including the skin and mucous membranes, that block foreign materials from entering the protected regions of the body.

Passive natural immunity   A form of borrowed immunity in which a person obtains antibodies made by another person, for example, the IgG molecules that cross the placenta from the mother to protect a baby or the ingestion of antibodies from a mother's breast milk.

Perforin   Proteins that lead to the formation of holes in cells.

Peyer's patches   Patches of lymphoid tissue found below the lining of the lower digestive track; they protect the body by secreting antibodies into the intestine.

Phagocytic cells   White blood cells with the ability to bind and engulf foreign materials.

Phagocytosis   The act of engulfing a solid, foreign object by a cell.

Plasma cell   Antibody-producing cell that develops from activated B cell.

Polymorphonuclear leukocyte   Granular white blood cells that have multiple staining regions.

Polysaccharide   A polymer made of repeating simple sugars.

SALT   See **Skin-associated lymphoid tissue**.

Skin-associated lymphoid tissue (SALT)   Tissues that serve as sites for the activation of B or T cells and that promote the secretion of antibodies (IgA) across the skin.

Suppressor T cells   Lymphoid white blood cells that help to suppress the immune response and are probably involved in selecting against B cells or T cells that would attack normal body cells.

T cell   A lymphoid white blood cell that matures in the thymus; the three major classes of T cells are T-helper cells, cytotoxic T cells, and suppressor T cells.

T-helper cells   T cells responsible for stimulation of both humoral (antibody-based) and cell-mediated immune responses; T-helper cells are the target of the HIV virus that causes AIDS.

Tear duct   An opening in the corner of the eye where tears are released.

Vaccination   The process of intentionally exposing a person to a foreign antigen with the hope that the resulting immune response will provide protection from that pathogen in the future.

Vaccine   Any material used to vaccinate. Common vaccines are live attenuated vaccines, killed cell vaccines, and vaccination with specific foreign antigens.

White blood cell   The family of blood cells that is essential to immune response.

Bibliography

Abbas, A. K., A. H. Lichtman, and D. L. Baker. *Basic Immunology: Functions and Disorders of the Immune System.* Philadelphia: Saunders Book Company, 2008

Atlas, R. *Many Faces—Many Microbes: Personal Reflections in Microbiology.* Washington, DC: ASM Press, 2000.

Edelson, E. *The Immune System.* Broomall, PA: Chelsea House Publishers, 2000.

Kindt, T. J. J., R. A Goldsby, and B. A. Osborne. *Kuby Immunology.* New York: W. H. Freeman Company, 2006.

Hyde, M. O., and E. H. Forsyth. *Vaccinations: From Smallpox to Cancer.* New York: Scholastic Library Publishing, 2000.

Ingraham, J. L., and C. A. Ingraham. *Introduction to Microbiology: A Case Study Approach.* Pacific Grove, CA: Brooks Cole Publishing, 2003.

Kaufmann, S. H., A. Sher, and R. Ahmed. *Immunology of Infectious Disease.* Washington, DC: ASM Press, 2002.

Latta, S. L. *Allergies.* Berkeley Heights, NJ: Enslow Publishers, Inc. 1998.

Male, D., J. Brostoff, D. Roth, and I. Roitt. *Immunology.* St. Louis, MO: Mosby, 2006.

Parham, P. *The Immune System.* London: Taylor and Francis, Inc., 2004.

Paul, W. E. *Fundamental Immunology.* New York: Lippincott Williams and Wilkins, 2008.

Playfair, J. H. L., and B. Chain. *Immunology at a Glance.* Hoboken, NJ: John Wiley and Sons, 2005

Sompayrac, L. *How the Immune System Works.* Hoboken, NJ: Wiley Blackwell, 2008.

Further Resources

Books

Balkwill, F., and M. Rolph. *Cell Wars*. Minneapolis: Lerner Publishing Group, 1994.

Epstein, H. *The Invisible Cure: Africa, the West, and the Fight Against AIDS*. New York: Farrar, Strauss, and Giroux, 2007.

Freidlander, M. P., and T. M. Phillips. *The Immune System: Your Body's Disease-Fighting Army*. Minneapolis: Lerner Publishing Group, 1998.

Edelson, E. *The Immune System*. Broomall, PA: Chelsea House Publishers, 2000.

Gonzales, D. *AIDS: Ten Stories of Courage*. Berkeley Heights, NJ: Enslow Publishers, Inc., 1996.

Hyde, M. O., and E. H. Forsyth. *Vaccinations: From Smallpox to Cancer*. New York: Scholastic Library Publishing, 2000.

Jussim, D. *AIDS and HIV: Risky Business*. Berkeley Heights, NJ: Enslow Publishers, Inc., 1997.

Latta, S. L. *Allergies*. Berkeley Heights, NJ: Enslow Publishers, Inc., 1998.

Nolen, S. *28: Stories of AIDS in Africa*. New York: Walker and Company, 2007.

Preston, R. *The Demon in the Freezer: A True Story*. New York: Random House, Inc., 2002.

Shilts, R. *And the Band Played On: Politics, People, and the AIDS Epidemic*. New York: St. Martin's Press, 1999.

Web Sites

Every Child By Two

www.ecbt.org/howdoim.htm

Immunization awareness organization with vaccine safety studies

Cells Alive

www.cellsalive.com/antibody.htm

Interactive description of B and T cell activation

Microbe eLibrary

*www.microbelibrary.org/images/suchman/htmlpages
immune_gif.html*

Interactive summary of phagocytosis

Microbe eLibrary

*www.microbelibrary.org/images/tterry/anim/phago053
html*

Video of the classical complement pathway

Picture Credits

Index

About the Author

Gregory J. Stewart completed his Ph.D. in microbiology at the University of California at Davis. His post-doctoral training was conducted at Exxon Research and Engineering and at E. I. DuPont de Nemours and Company. He spent seven years at the University of South Florida as an assistant and associate professor of Biology. In 1993, he joined the Biology Department of the University of West Georgia (formerly West Georgia College), where he served as professor and department chair for eight years. After one year as assistant dean of Arts and Sciences at West Georgia, Stewart accepted a senior fellowship with the Bureau of Arms Control of the U.S. Department of State. He served as Senior Microbiologist for the Bureau of International Security and Nonproliferation at the State Department. His duties included scientific and technical support to the Biological and Toxins Weapons Convention (an international treaty), an advisor to the U.S. Department of State and other U.S. agencies on issues related to microbiology, biological weapons reduction, bioterrorism and counterterrorism threat reduction and response, and issues of biosafety and biosecurity of dangerous pathogenic microorganisms. Stewart has collaborated with both domestic and international organizations on the development of standards for biosafety and pathogen security. He served as a reviewer for the Interagency Select Agent Advisory Group for the National Institutes of Health and for several other national agencies. Stewart is currently a principal scientist with Applied Systems Research, Inc. He is the author of more than 30 scientific publications. Stewart lives with his wife, Patricia, a clinical microbiologist, and is the stepfather of three grown children and the grandfather of four.